W9-AMB-722

The
SmartCook
Collection

Soup

The SmartCook Collection

Soup

LONDON, NEW YORK, MUNICH,
MELBOURNE, and DELHI

Senior Editor   Anja Schmidt
Art Director   Dirk Kaufman
Designer   Bill Miller
Design Assistant   Adrian Peters
DTP Coordinator   Kathy Farias
Production Manager   Ivor Parker
Executive Managing Editor   Sharon Lucas
Publisher   Carl Raymond

U.S. Recipe Adapter   Rick Rodgers

First published in 2004 by BBC Books
BBC Worldwide Limited
Woodlands, 80 Wood Lane
London W12 0TT

Published in the United States in 2006 by
DK Publishing
375 Hudson Street,
New York, New York 10014

06 07 08 09 10 10 9 8 7 6 5 4 3 2 1

A proportion of these recipes has been
published previously in *Delia Smith's Winter
Collection, Delia Smith's Summer Collection,
Delia's How To Cook Books One, Two*, and *Three,
Delia Smith's Complete Illustrated Cookery
Course, Delia Smith's Christmas, Delia's Red Nose
Collection*, and *Delia's Vegetarian Collection.*

A catalog record for this book is available from
the Library of Congress.

ISBN 0-7566-1923-8

Printed and bound in China by Toppan Printing
Co., (Shenzen) Ltd.
Color separation by Radstock Reproduction Ltd
Midsomer Norton
Additional color work by Colourscan, Singapore

Cover and title-page photographs: Michael Paul
For further photographic credits, see page 136

Some recipes in this book contain raw eggs,
which are know to contain the potentially harmful
salmonella bacterium. Do not serve dishes made
with raw eggs to the very young, elderly, or
those with compromised immune systems.

Discover more at **www.dk.com**

Introduction

When I look back over my years of cookbook writing, I have to admit that very often, decisions about what to do have sprung from what my own particular needs are. As a very busy person, who has to work, run a home, and cook, I felt it was extremely useful to have, for instance, summer recipes in one book – likewise winter and Christmas – giving easy access to those specific seasons.

The SmartCook Collection has come about for similar reasons. Thirty-three years of recipe writing have produced literally thousands of recipes. So I now feel what would be really helpful is to create a kind of ordered library (so I don't have to rack my brains and wonder which book this or that recipe is in!). Thus, if I want to make a soup, I don't have to look through the soup sections of various books, but have all the recipes in one convenient collection. Similarly, if I've managed to get hold of some veal shanks, I can go straight for the Italian collection, and so on.

In compiling these collections, I have chosen what I think are the best and most popular recipes and, at the same time, have added some that are completely new. It is my hope that those who have not previously tried my recipes will now have smaller collections to sample, and that those dedicated followers will appreciate an ordered library to provide easy access and a reminder of what has gone before and may have been forgotten.

Delia Smith

Conversion Tables

All these are approximate conversions, which have either been rounded up or down. In a few recipes it has been necessary to modify them very slightly. Never mix metric and imperial measures in one recipe; stick to one system or the other.

All spoon measurements used throughout this book are level unless specified otherwise.

All butter is salted unless specified otherwise.

All recipes have been double-tested, using a standard convection oven.

Weights	
½ oz	10 g
¾	20
1	25
1½	40
2	50
2½	60
3	75
4	110
4½	125
5	150
6	175
7	200
8	225
9	250
10	275
12	350
1 lb	450
1 lb 8 oz	700
2	900
3	1.35 kg

Volume	
2 fl oz	55 ml
3	75
5 (¼ pint)	150
10 (½ pint)	275
1 pint	570
1¼	725
1¾	1 litre
2	1.2
2½	1.5
4	2.25

Dimensions	
⅛ inch	3 mm
¼	5
½	1 cm
¾	2
1	2.5
1¼	3
1½	4
1¾	4.5
2	5
2½	6
3	7.5
3½	9
4	10
5	13
5¼	13.5
6	15
6½	16
7	18
7½	19
8	20
9	23
9½	24
10	25.5
11	28
12	30

Oven temperatures		
Gas mark 1	275°F	140°C
2	300	150
3	325	170
4	350	180
5	375	190
6	400	200
7	425	220
8	450	230
9	475	240

Contents

Spring

Italian Minestrone with Pasta
Serves 6

2 tablespoons butter

1 tablespoon olive oil

2 oz sliced bacon or pancetta, finely chopped

1 medium onion, finely chopped

2 medium celery ribs, finely chopped

2 medium carrots, finely chopped

2 ripe medium tomatoes, peeled and chopped

1 garlic clove, crushed through a press

9 cups Chicken Stock or Vegetable Stock (page 128)

salt and freshly ground black pepper to taste

2 small leeks

2 cups finely shredded cabbage

½ cup tube-shaped short pasta, such as ditalini

1 tablespoon tomato paste

2 tablespoons chopped fresh parsley

1½ tablespoons chopped fresh basil

Lots of freshly grated Parmesan, for serving

If you have a food processor, it makes very light work of chopping the vegetables – but use the pulse button so you don't chop them too small. For something different, you can replace the macaroni with Italian risotto rice. Either way, serve it with lots of freshly grated Parmesan.

1. First of all, heat the butter and oil in a large saucepan. Add the bacon and cook for a couple of minutes. Add the onion, followed by the celery and carrots and then the tomatoes, cooking each for a minute or two before adding the next one. Now stir in the crushed garlic and some salt and pepper. Cover and cook very gently for 20 minutes or so to allow the vegetables to cook in their own juices – give it an occasional stir to prevent the vegetables from sticking. Pour in the stock, bring to a boil, and simmer gently, covered, for about 1 hour.

2. To prepare the leeks, first cut off and discard the tough, dark green tops. Make a vertical split about halfway down the center of each one and clean them by rinsing under the cold running water as you fan out the layers – this will rid them of any hidden dust and grit. Then finely chop the leeks.

3. When the hour is up, stir the leeks, cabbage, pasta, and tomato paste into the soup. Cook uncovered for another 10 minutes or until the pasta is done. Finally, stir in the parsley and basil. Serve the minestrone in warmed soup bowls, sprinkled with Parmesan cheese.

Scallop Bisque
Serves 4 to 6

4 tablespoons butter

1 medium onion, finely chopped

2 large baking potatoes (1 lb), such as russet or Burbank, peeled and diced

salt and freshly ground black pepper to taste

2½ cups Fish Stock (page 128), heated

12 oz scallops, with or without roe

1¼ cups milk

2 large egg yolks

⅓ cup heavy cream

Croutons (page 129), for serving

Chopped fresh parsley, for garnish

This really is one of the most luxurious and delicate soups imaginable. It is very easy to prepare and cook, but perfect for a special occasion.

1. First, melt the butter in a fairly large saucepan over very low heat. Add the onion and cook very gently without coloring at all, about 10 minutes. Next, add the diced potatoes, mix well, and season with salt and pepper. Keeping the heat very low, put the lid on the saucepan and let the vegetables slowly cook in their juices for another 10 to 15 minutes. After that pour in the stock, give it a good stir, cover the pan again, and simmer gently over medium-low heat until the vegetables are tender, 10 to 15 minutes.

2. Meanwhile, you prepare the scallops: rinse and dry them thoroughly. If the coral-colored roe is attached, remove and chop it, and set it aside. Roughly dice the white parts of the scallop, and put them in a saucepan with the milk and a little salt and pepper. Cook very gently over medium-low heat for 3 to 4 minutes, or until the scallops are opaque.

3. When the vegetables are tender, in batches, transfer them and their cooking liquid to a blender or food processor and purée. Now combine the scallops and their milk with the potato purée. The soup can be made up to this point, cooled, and refrigerated, a few hours before serving. Reheat gently over very low heat before proceeding.

4. When you are ready to serve the soup, beat the egg yolks thoroughly with the cream in a small bowl. Remove the soup from the heat, and stir a large spoonful of the soup into the yolk mixture. Stir this into the soup. Return the saucepan to gentle heat and cook, stirring, until the soup thickens slightly – but be very careful not to let it come anywhere near the boil or it will curdle.

5. To serve the soup, ladle it into warm soup bowls and garnish with croutons and some chopped fresh parsley.

Spring Asparagus Soup
Serves 6

2 lb asparagus

4 tablespoons butter

1 medium onion, finely chopped

4 teaspoons all-purpose flour

1 quart Chicken Stock (page 128), heated

salt and freshly ground black pepper to taste

⅔ cup heavy cream or crème fraîche

This elegant soup is perfect to make when asparagus comes into season in spring. It can be served hot or very well chilled.

1. Prepare the asparagus by cutting away and discarding the tough, stringy ends of the stalks. Cut off and reserve 12 asparagus tips to garnish the soup. Now chop the remaining trimmed stalks into 1 inch lengths.

2. Next, melt the butter in a large saucepan over a low heat. Add the onion and cook for 5 minutes, keeping the heat low to prevent the onion from coloring. Stir in the asparagus, then cover and let the vegetables cook in their own juices for about 10 minutes, giving them a stir now and then.

3. Sprinkle the vegetables with the flour, and stir well to soak up the juices. Stir in the stock, a little at a time. When all the stock has been added, bring the soup to a simmer. Season with salt and pepper, and keeping the heat low, let the soup barely simmer, partially covered, until the asparagus is very tender, for 20 to 25 minutes.

4. Now you need to let the soup cool a little. Pour it into a blender or food processor and blend in batches (a large bowl to hold the puréed soup is helpful here). Taste to check the seasoning. Return the soup to the saucepan. Stir in the cream or crème fraîche and the reserved asparagus tips. Reheat gently to warm the asparagus tips through, 3 to 4 minutes. Serve very hot in warm soup bowls. Or, alternatively, cool and chill thoroughly and serve in chilled bowls.

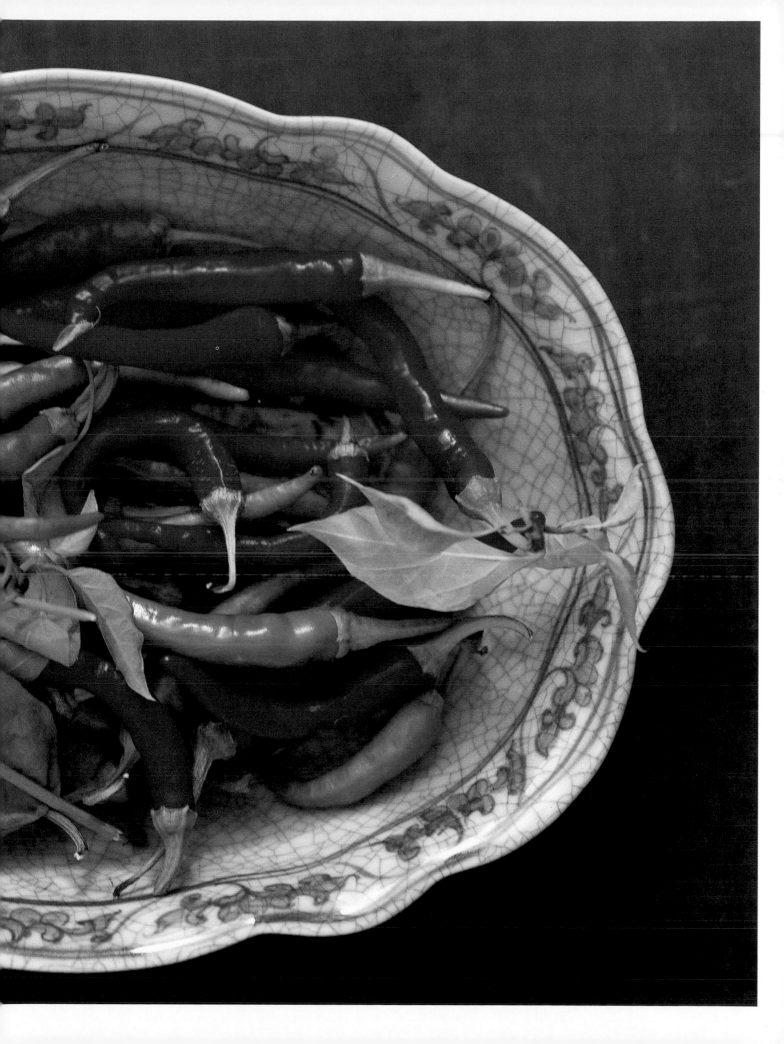

Chickpea Soup with Fresh Chilis and Cilantro
Serves 4 to 6

1 cup dried chickpeas (garbanzo beans), soaked overnight in enough cold water to cover by 2 inches

1 tablespoon coriander seeds

1 tablespoon cumin seeds

4 tablespoons butter

6 plump garlic cloves, finely chopped

3 small fresh red chilies, such as serrano, seeded, 2 halved and 1 finely shredded

1 teaspoon ground turmeric

8 large sprigs fresh cilantro, leaves finely chopped, stalks reserved

1 lemon, zest grated and juiced (2–3 tablespoons lemon juice)

1 cup crème fraîche or heavy cream

salt and freshly ground black pepper to taste

This has decidedly Mexican overtones. It isn't too hot and spicy but the presence of the chilies does give it a nice kick, and the flavor and texture of chickpeas is perfect for soup.

1. First of all, drain the soaked chickpeas in a colander and rinse them under cold water. Place them in a large saucepan with 6½ cups boiling, water. Bring them to a simmer, cover, and cook very gently for about 1 hour or until the chickpeas are absolutely tender.

2. While they're cooking, prepare the rest of the soup ingredients. Dry-roast the coriander and cumin seeds in a small preheated skillet for 2 to 3 minutes, or until they are fragrant. Crush them in a pestle and mortar.

3. After that, melt the butter in the pan, add the crushed coriander and cumin, along with the chopped garlic and 2 halved chilies, and cook over a low heat for about 5 minutes. Now add the turmeric, stir, and heat gently for a minute or so before removing the skillet from the heat.

4. As soon as the chickpeas are tender, drain them in a colander placed over a bowl to reserve the cooking water. Transfer the chickpeas and a couple of ladles of cooking water to a blender or food processor, and purée them until fine and smooth. Now add the lemon zest, cilantro stalks, and butter-spice mixture from the skillet, along with another ladleful of cooking water, and blend again.

5. Next, return the chickpea purée to the saucepan, and stir in the remaining cooking water. Bring it all to a gentle simmer, give it a good stir, season, then simmer gently for another 30 minutes. All this can be done in advance. When you're ready to serve, reheat it very gently without letting it come to a boil. Stir in half of the crème fraîche and the lemon juice. Check the seasoning, then serve in hot soup bowls with the remaining crème fraîche swirled in. Scatter with the shredded chilies and chopped cilantro leaves before serving.

Bloody Mary Soup
Serves 4 to 6

4 ripe medium tomatoes

4½ cups tomato juice, preferably organic

1½ tablespoons Worcestershire sauce

1½ tablespoons balsamic vinegar

Juice of 2 limes

8 drops of hot red pepper sauce

Salt and freshly ground black pepper to taste

For the salsa

2 ripe medium tomatoes (from above)

1 small celery rib

1½ tablespoons vodka

¼ teaspoon celery salt

4 dashes of hot red pepper sauce, or more to taste

While this tasty soup is actually more of a Virgin Mary, there is a dash of vodka in the accompanying salsa. If you feel like it, spike the soup with more vodka just before serving. The salsa isn't essential, and you can garnish the soup with a spoonful of yogurt, some watercress, and a sprinkle of finely chopped celery as an alternative.

1. Place the tomatoes in a heatproof bowl and pour boiling water over them. Let stand for 1 minute. Drain the tomatoes, and slip off the skins (protecting your hands with a kitchen towel, if necessary). Set aside 2 tomatoes for the salsa. Cut the remaining 2 tomatoes in half, squeeze out the seeds, and chop them very finely. Place the tomatoes in a large saucepan. Bring the tomatoes to a gentle simmer and let them cook until heated through, about 3 minutes. Next, pour in the tomato juice, the Worcestershire sauce, vinegar, lime juice, and hot pepper sauce, and season with salt and pepper. Do a bit of tasting here – it might need a dash more red pepper sauce or another squeeze of lime. The soup can be made ahead to this point.

2. Now, to make the salsa, cut the reserved tomatoes in half, then squeeze out the seeds and dice the flesh. Finely chop the celery. Mix the tomatoes and celery with the vodka, celery salt, and red pepper sauce.

3. When you're ready to serve, return the soup to a simmer. Ladle it into warm soup bowls and spoon the salsa on top. On diet days I like to serve this soup with rye crackers.

Smoked Fish Chowder
with Poached Quail Eggs
Serves 4

1 lb 4 oz finnan haddie (smoked haddock, available at specialty grocers or by mail order) cut into 4 pieces

2¼ cups milk

freshly ground black pepper to taste

1 bay leaf

3 tablespoons butter

1 medium onion, finely chopped

¼ cup all-purpose flour

1 tablespoon fresh lemon juice

1 tablespoon chopped fresh flat-leaf parsley

salt to taste

4 eggs, preferably quail

Smoked haddock makes a very fine soup, and this recipe is adapted from a famous version invented in Scotland, where it is called Cullen Skink. If you add eggs to the soup, this makes a delightful surprise as you lift up an egg on your spoon. Serve in warmed, shallow soup bowls with whole-wheat bread and butter.

1. Start by placing the haddock pieces in a large medium saucepan with the milk and 2¼ cups water. Season with pepper (but no salt yet) and add the bay leaf. Now gently bring it to a simmer and simmer very gently for 5 minutes. Remove from the heat, pour the fish and liquid into a bowl, and let stand for 15 minutes.

2. Meanwhile, wipe out the saucepan with paper towels. Melt the butter in the saucepan, add the onion, and cook very slowly, without browning, for about 10 minutes. Remove the haddock from the liquid with a slotted spoon, transfer to a board, peel off the skin, and flake the fish. Discard the bay leaf. Next, stir the flour into the onion to soak up the juices, then gradually stir in the reserved fish-cooking liquid. When that's all in, add half the flaked haddock. Now allow the soup to cool a little, then pour it into a blender or food processor and blend to a purée. After that, pass it through a sieve back into the saucepan, pressing through any solid bits of fish through the sieve, to extract all the flavor. Discard any solids in the sieve. Add the remaining flaked haddock to the soup. Taste it and season with salt, pepper, and lemon juice, and keep warm on very low heat.

3. Now poach the eggs: half-fill a skillet with water and bring to a gentle simmer – there should be the merest trace of bubbles simmering on the base of the pan. Break the 4 eggs into the water and let them cook for just 1 minute. Turn off the heat and let the eggs stand in the water for 10 minutes, after which time the whites will be set and the yolks creamy. Using a slotted spoon, place the eggs on folded paper towels to drain briefly. Place 1 egg in each warmed serving bowl, ladle in the soup, and serve, sprinkled with the chopped parsley.

Shiitake Soup with Rice and Sesame Toast
Serves 6

½ oz dried shiitake mushrooms (about 6 mushrooms)

4 tablespoons white miso dissolved in 7 cups boiling water

8 oz shiitake mushrooms, stems discarded

3 oz cremini mushrooms

1 tablespoon peanut or other flavorless oil

2 medium onions, finely chopped

2 tablespoons basmati rice

1½ tablespoons cornstarch

2 scallions, white and green parts, finely chopped

salt and freshly ground black pepper to taste

For the sesame toast

6 medium-thick slices cut from a whole loaf of firm white sandwich bread, crusts trimmed

3 tablespoons butter, softened

¼ cup sesame seeds

This is a lovely light soup, without too many calories, made with miso and dried shiitake mushrooms, which have a rich flavor. You can also just use fresh shiitake mushrooms, if you prefer.

1. First of all, rinse the dried mushrooms in a sieve under cold water, then place them in a heatproof bowl. Add 2 cups of the hot miso mixture and set aside to soak and soften for about 30 minutes. Meanwhile, finely chop the fresh shiitake and cremini mushrooms. Line a wire sieve with a double layer of moistened paper towels and place it over a bowl. Strain the soaked mushrooms in the sieve, squeezing them to extract any excess liquid, and reserve the soaking liquid. Chop the soaked mushrooms fairly finely. Heat the oil in a large saucepan, add the onions, and cook gently for about 10 minutes or until softened. Next, stir in the fresh and the soaked mushrooms, and cook for a minute or two. Pour in the mushroom soaking liquid and the remaining miso mixture and bring to a simmer. Stir in the rice. Simmer gently, uncovered, stirring occasionally to prevent the rice from sticking, for 20 to 25 minutes or until the rice is just tender.

2. Meanwhile, you can start to make the sesame toast. Preheat the broiler. Then toast the slices of bread in the broiler on one side only. Now spread them with the softened butter on the untoasted side, right up to the edges. Sprinkle the sesame seeds over each slice to cover as evenly as possible, pressing the seeds down so they will stay in position.

3. Toward the end of the soup's cooking time, in a small bowl, mix the cornstarch (which will thicken the soup) with 2 tablespoons of cold water until smooth. Then, when the soup is ready, stir in the dissolved cornstarch, together with three-quarters of the scallions and, stirring constantly, bring back to a simmer and cook for 1 minute. Season to taste. To finish making the toast, return the bread, sesame-encrusted sides up, to the grill. Toast until the seeds are lightly toasted and the bread turns golden brown. Then cut each slice up into four squares and eat immediately with the piping hot soup, garnished with the remaining scallions.

Coriander-Scented Carrot Soup
Serves 6

1 tablespoon coriander seeds

2 tablespoons butter

2 lb carrots, peeled and chopped

1 small garlic clove, crushed through a press

5 cups Chicken Stock or Vegetable Stock (page 128)

3 tablespoons chopped fresh cilantro, plus 6 small sprigs for garnish

2 tablespoons crème fraîche or heavy cream, plus more for garnish

salt and freshly ground black pepper to taste

This is a lovely soup to make with spring carrots, which are not quite as sweet as those in the summer. Coriander is said to have the flavor of roasted orange peel, which makes the two perfect partners. Serve the soup with plenty of warm crusty bread.

1. Begin by dry-roasting the coriander seeds in a small skillet over medium heat, stirring and tossing them around for 1 to 2 minutes, or until they begin to look toasted and start to jump in the pan. Place them in a mortar and crush them coarsely.

2. Next, heat the butter in a large saucepan, then add the carrots, garlic, and three-quarters of the crushed coriander seeds. Stir well, then cover the saucepan and let the vegetables cook over gentle heat until they begin to soften – about 10 minutes.

3. Next, add the stock, season with salt and pepper, and bring everything to a boil. Then reduce the heat to low and simmer for 15 to 20 minutes, partially covered, or until the vegetables are tender. Let the soup cool a little, then purée it in batches in a blender or food processor (a large bowl to hold each batch of puréed soup is helpful here). After that, return the purée to the saucepan and stir in the chopped cilantro and 2 tablespoons of the crème fraîche. Reheat the soup, then taste to check the seasoning, and serve in warmed bowls. Garnish each one with a swirl of crème fraîche, a sprinkling of the remaining toasted coriander seeds, and a sprig of fresh coriander.

Roasted Tomato Soup with Basil Purée and Olive Croutons
Serves 4

1 lb 8 oz ripe medium red tomatoes, skinned and halved crosswise (see page 18 for peeling instructions)

3–4 tablespoons extra virgin olive oil

1 plump garlic clove, chopped

About 30 large sprigs fresh basil

1 small baking potato, such as russet or Burbank (about 4 oz)

1½ teaspoons tomato paste

1 teaspoon balsamic vinegar

salt and freshly ground black pepper to taste

Olive Croutons (page 129), for serving

At first you're going to think, "Why bother to roast tomatoes just for soup?" But once you've tasted the difference you'll know it's worth it – especially outside of the summer tomato season when it's difficult to find really ripe, full-flavored tomatoes. And roasting really isn't any trouble, it just means time in the oven.

1. Preheat the oven to 375°F. Arrange the tomatoes, cut sides up, on a baking sheet and season with salt and pepper. Sprinkle a few droplets of olive oil on each one, followed by the chopped garlic, and finally, top each one with a piece of basil leaf (dipping the basil in oil first to get a good coating). Now pop it into the oven and roast the tomatoes for 50 minutes to 1 hour or until the edges are slightly blackened – what happens in this process is that the liquid in the tomatoes evaporates and concentrates their flavor, as do the toasted edges. If you wish, roast a few whole small garlic cloves with the tomatoes, and skip the chopped garlic. About 20 minutes before the end of the roasting time, peel and chop the potato, place it in a saucepan with 2 cups lightly salted boiling water and the tomato paste, and simmer until tender, about 20 minutes.

2. When the tomatoes are ready, scrape them with all their juices and crusty leftover pieces into a blender or food processor (a spatula is best for this). If you have roasted whole garlic cloves, squeeze the tender garlic from the skin into the blender. When the potato and its liquid have cooled a little, add these, too, and process everything into a not-too-uniform purée. If you wish, pass the soup through a wire sieve to remove the seeds but I prefer to leave them in, because I like the texture. Return the soup to the saucepan. Just before serving the soup – which should be reheated very gently – make the basil purée by stripping the remaining leaves into a mortar, sprinkling with ¼ teaspoon of salt, then bashing the leaves down with the pestle. It takes a minute or two for the leaves to break down and become a purée, at which point add 2 tablespoons of olive oil and the balsamic vinegar and stir well. Or, purée the basil, salt, oil, and vinegar in a blender or food processor. Serve each bowl of soup garnished with a swirl of the basil purée and a few olive croutons.

Spinach Soup with Melting Fontina Cheese
Serves 4 to 6

4 tablespoons butter

2 medium baking potatoes, such as russet or Burbank, peeled and cut into ½-inch cubes (about 14 oz)

2 shallots, chopped

3 cups Vegetable Stock (page 128)

15 oz fresh spinach leaves, tough stems removed, well rinsed (about 10 packed cups)

A generous grating of fresh nutmeg

Salt and freshly ground black pepper to taste

1 cup crème fraîche or heavy cream

3 oz Italian Fontina or Gruyère cheese, cut into ¼-inch dice (about ¾ cup)

chopped fresh parsley or finely chopped fresh chives, for garnish

Italian Fontina cheese, which has a melting creaminess, is the best to use in this soup, but if you can't get hold of it, substitute shredded Gruyère.

1. Begin by melting the butter in a large saucepan and then add the potatoes and shallots. Stir everything together, then cover the saucepan and cook them very gently for 10 minutes. Next, add the stock and bring to the simmer. Let everything simmer for about 10 minutes or until the potato is tender. Now add the spinach leaves, cover with a lid, and allow them to wilt in the heat of the pan. Then stir everything together, add a generous grating of fresh nutmeg, and season with salt and pepper. Once all the spinach has wilted, take the pan off the heat, leave it aside to cool a little, then purée the soup in batches in a blender or food processor until smooth (have a bowl ready to put the puréed soup in).

2. Then return the soup to the saucepan and stir in the crème fraîche. When you're ready to serve the soup, reheat it gently just up to a simmer, and finally stir in the diced cheese. Ladle the hot soup into warm bowls and, if you like, garnish each one with a scattering of chopped parsley or chives.

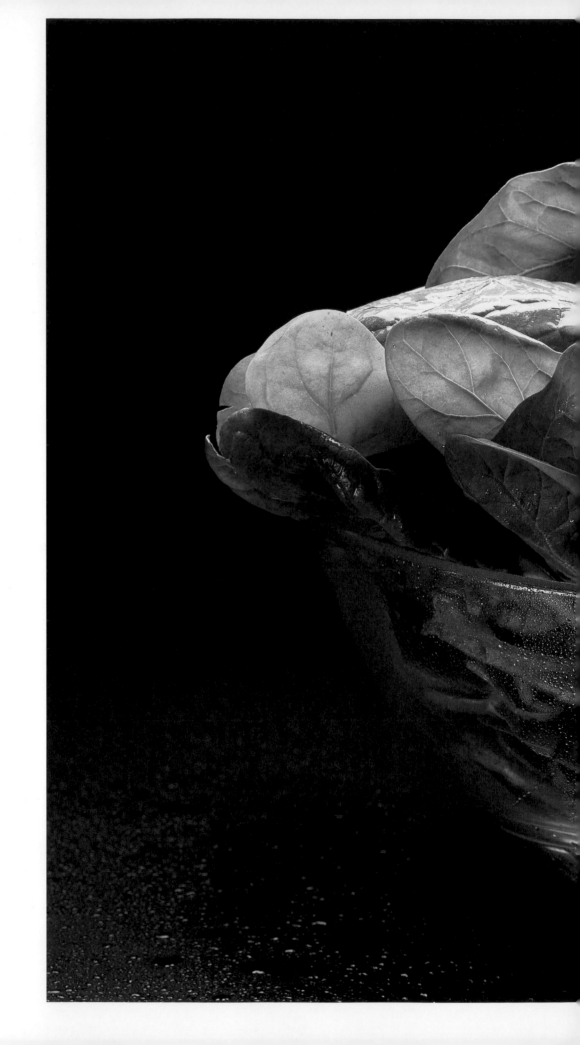

Tart and Spicy Thai Chicken-Vegetable Soup
Serves 4

About 20 sprigs fresh cilantro

2 small red Thai or serrano chilies

4½ cups Chicken Stock (page 128)

1 stalk of lemon grass, outer layers removed, tender bulb coarsely chopped

A 1-inch piece of fresh ginger, peeled and sliced

2 medium, ripe tomatoes

2 boneless and skinless chicken breasts (6 oz each)

3 scallions, white and green parts

½ cup shelled fresh peas

½ cup sugar snap peas, cut in half

1 tablespoon Thai fish sauce

1 tablespoon tamarind concentrate

Juice of a large lime (about 2 tablespoons)

Lemon grass, tamarind, and lime add a complex tartness to this delightfully spicy soup. Tamarind concentrate is available at Asian grocers. If you can't find it, add a bit more lime juice. Althought the broth is light, each bowl is chockfull of a variety of complex vegetables, so while this is suggested as a first course for 4, it could serve as a fine lunch or light supper for 2 or 3 people.

1. First of all, you need to pick all the cilantro leaves off the stalks. Cut 1 of the chilies in half lengthwise and remove the seeds. Next, put the chicken stock into a large saucepan and add the coriander stalks, halved chili, lemon grass, and ginger. Bring the mixture to a boil, give everything a stir, then cover and simmer very gently for 15 minutes to allow the Thai flavors to infuse the stock. You can make this stock in advance but add the rest of the ingredients shortly before serving.

2. Meanwhile, place the tomatoes in a bowl, pour boiling water over them, and let stand for 1 minute before draining. Next, skin the tomatoes and cut each one into quarters. Remove the seeds and cut each quarter into thirds lengthwise, so you end up with thin slices. Now cut each chicken breast in half crosswise and then slice each half into five or six long thin strips. Slice each of these in half lengthways so you end up with thin slivers of chicken. Now strain the stock into a colander set over a bowl and discard the solids. Next, return the stock to the saucepan and bring it back to a simmer. Stir in the chicken and half of the scallions. Stir, cover again, and gently poach the chicken for 5 minutes or until it is cooked through. Meanwhile, trim and halve the remaining chili, remove the seeds, and then finely slice it, making sure you wash your hands afterwards.

3. Next, add the peas, sugar snaps, sliced chili, fish sauce, tamarind, and lime juice to the soup, stir, and gently simmer for 2 to 3 minutes or until the peas are just tender but still retain their bite. Stir in the slices of tomato at the last minute. Divide the cilantro leaves among four deep bowls. Ladle the piping hot soup on top, sprinkle with the remaining scallions, and serve immediately.

Summer

Summer

White Gazpacho with Almonds and Green Grapes
Serves 4

1¾ cups natural almonds, preferably Spanish almonds (never use preblanched almonds for this recipe)

About 1 cup olive oil, preferably Spanish

3 garlic cloves

2 teaspoons sherry vinegar

2 teaspoons salt, or more, to taste

To serve

8 ice cubes

1 cup halved and seeded black or green grapes

1 sweet apple, such as Golden Delicious, peeled, cored, and thinly sliced

This wonderful Andalusian recipe is laced with garlic. It's served ice cold – ice cubes are added to the cold soup at the last minute – and can be made up to five days ahead. In fact, it improves upon standing.

1. First, you need to blanch the almonds. To do this, place them in a heatproof bowl, pour in enough boiling water to cover, then set aside for 3 to 4 minutes. Now drain them in a colander and simply squeeze the nuts out of their skins into the bowl.

2. After that, put the almonds in a blender or food processor and pour in the olive oil. (The oil should just cover the almonds – if it doesn't, add a little more.) Then peel and add the garlic, the vinegar, and salt, and process until everything is smooth. Now, with the motor still running, slowly add about 1½ cups cold water. Pour the soup into a large bowl. If it seems too thick, add a little more water. Then cover the bowl with plastic wrap and refrigerate until you're ready to serve.

3. Just before serving, stir in the ice cubes. Ladle the soup into chilled bowls. Garnish with the grapes and apple slices and serve immediately.

Green Garden Soup
Serves 4

6 tablespoons butter

2 medium baking potatoes
(12 oz), such as russet or
Burbank, peeled and finely diced

4 or 5 scallions, white and green
parts, finely chopped

1 small round lettuce, such as
bibb, rinsed, patted dry, cored,
and shredded

1 kirby cucumber, scrubbed,
seeded, and chopped (no need
to peel)

3⅓ cups Chicken Stock or
Vegetable Stock (page 128)

Salt and freshly ground black
pepper to taste

Snipped fresh chives, to garnish

This is a helpful recipe for gardeners whose summer crop of vegetables threatens to overwhelm them. If you like, you can serve this soup cold in chilled bowls in really hot weather. Either way, it is a lovely soup to serve on a summer's day.

1. First of all, in a medium saucepan, melt the butter gently, then add the potatoes, scallions, lettuce, and cucumber. Stir everything in the butter, then, keeping the heat very low, cover and let cook gently for 10 minutes.

2. Now stir in the stock, add some salt and pepper, and bring a boil over high heat, and cover again. Reduce the heat to low and simmer gently until the potatoes are very tender, about 20 minutes. Let the soup cool a little, then purée in batches in a blender or food processor, pouring the puréed soup into a large bowl. Finally, check the seasoning and gently reheat the soup in the saucepan. Serve it with the freshly snipped chives stirred in at the last moment or sprinkle a few into each bowl.

Spanish Gazpacho
Serves 6

1 lb 8 oz ripe, firm tomatoes

2 or 3 scallions, white and green parts, chopped

1 kirby cucumber, scrubbed, seeded, and chopped

½ large red or green bell pepper, seeds and ribs removed, chopped

2 garlic cloves, crushed in a press

1¼ teaspoons chopped fresh basil, marjoram, or thyme (depending on what's available)

¼ cup olive oil

1½ tablespoons wine vinegar

Salt and freshly ground black pepper to taste

For the garnish

½ large red or green pepper, seeds and ribs removed, very finely chopped

½ medium cucumber, peeled, seeded, and finely chopped

2 scallions, white and green parts, finely chopped

1 hard-boiled egg, finely chopped

1½ tablespoons chopped fresh parsley

salt and freshly ground black pepper to taste

To serve

½ cup olive oil

2 slices firm white bread, cut into ½-inch cubes

4 ice cubes

Strictly for summer when tomatoes and the other vegetables that make up this uncooked soup are at their peak, gazpacho is a great choice to begin almost any warm-weather meal. The trick is balancing the puréed base with the finely diced garnish that adorns the top. Olive oil-crisped croutons finish off this great Spanish classic.

1. Begin by placing the tomatoes in a bowl and pouring boiling water over them. Let stand for a minute and then the skins will loosen and slip off very easily (protect your hands with a cloth, if necessary). Halve the tomatoes, scoop out and discard the seeds, and roughly chop the flesh.

2. Now combine the tomatoes, scallion, cucumber, bell pepper, garlic, and herbs in a bowl. Mix the oil, vinegar, and a seasoning of salt and pepper in a measuring cup. In batches, purée the vegetables and the oil mixture in a blender or food processor, and pour the purée into a large bowl. Taste to check the seasoning and stir in a little cold water to thin it slightly – anything from ⅓ to ⅔ cup. Cover the bowl and refrigerate until chilled.

3. To make the garnish, simply mix all the ingredients in a bowl and season with salt and pepper.

4. To make croutons for the soup, heat the oil in a medium skillet over high heat until the oil shimmers. Add the bread cubes and fry until they are golden brown, about 1 minute. Use a slotted spoon to transfer them to paper towels to drain and cool. Serve the soup chilled with 4 ice cubes floating in the tureen or set on a bed of ice. Pass the chopped vegetables at the table, together with the croutons.

Creamy Potato Soup with Wilted Greens

Serves 6

6 tablespoons butter

4 medium baking potatoes
(1 lb 8 oz), such as russet or
Burbank, peeled and diced

3 medium onions (1 pound),
chopped

3⅓ cups Chicken Stock or
Vegetable Stock (page 128)

1¼ cups milk

Salt and freshly ground black
pepper to taste

4 oz mixed field greens (mesclun)

To save time with this soup, you could use the combination of mixed field greens (often called mesclun) available at many markets. Be sure your mix includes a good amount of so-called bitter greens, such as watercress, baby spinach, and arugula, and not just sweet lettuce varieties. Russet potatoes are mealy and fall apart when cooked. That is why they are often used for mashed potatoes, and why they are a good a good choice here, since the soup base is puréed.

1. In a large, heavy-bottomed saucepan, gently melt 4 tablespoons of the butter. Add the potatoes and onions, stirring them all around with a wooden spoon so they get a nice coating of butter. Season with salt and pepper, then cover and let the vegetables cook gently over very low heat for about 15 minutes, stirring everything now and then.

2. After that, add the stock and milk, bring to a simmer, cover, and let the soup simmer very gently for 20 minutes or until the potatoes are soft   be careful because, if you have the heat too high, the milk may make the soup boil over.

3. Now let the soup cool a little, then purée it in batches in a blender or food processor, pouring the puréed soup into a large bowl. Return the soup to the saucepan, then gently reheat it, tasting to check the seasoning.

4. Meanwhile, roughly chop the mesclun, and stir the leaves into the soup with the remaining 2 tablespoons butter. As soon as the leaves have wilted, serve the soup in warm bowls.

Vichyssoise with Lemon Grass and Cilantro
Serves 4

30 large fresh cilantro sprigs

4 lemon grass stalks

5 scallions

4 tablespoons butter

2 medium onions, chopped

2 medium baking potatoes (10 oz), such as russet or Burbanks, peeled and finely diced

⅔ cup milk

Salt and freshly ground black pepper to taste

To serve

4 ice cubes, for serving

Thin lemon slices, for garnish

Leeks, which have made vichyssoise famous, are not at their best in summer, but this alternative version is, I think, even better. In hot summer weather it's lovely made with fresh lemon grass, available in Asian specialty shops and larger supermarkets. Remember to serve the soup icy cold in chilled soup bowls.

1. First of all, strip the leaves from the cilantro sprigs, reserving the stems and finely chop the leaves to use as a garnish. Lemon grass is dealt with in a similar way to leeks: that is, you trim the root and cut off the tough top part; set the tops aside. Peel off the thick outer skin to reveal the tender bulb, and add this skin to the tops. Finely chop the bulb and set aside. Now coarsely chop 4 of the scallions, and finely chop and reserve the remaining scallion for garnish. Next, combine the cilantro stems, lemon grass trimmings, and coarsely chopped scallions in a large saucepan with 3½ cups water and some salt. Simmer the soup, covered, for about 30 minutes to make a stock.

2. To make the soup, begin by melting the butter in a large saucepan, then add the chopped lemon grass, onions, and potatoes, and cover. Cook gently over low heat for about 10 minutes. After that, pour in the stock through a strainer, discard the solids, then add the milk and about three-quarters of the cilantro leaves. Season with salt and pepper, bring the soup up to a simmer, and simmer very gently over low heat, partially covered, until the potatoes are very tender, about 25 minutes.

3. Let the soup cool a little before puréeing it in batches in a blender or food processor. Pour it through a strainer into a bowl. Let the soup cool thoroughly, then cover and refrigerate until chilled.

4. I think it's a good idea to serve the soup in glass bowls that have already been chilled. Add a cube of ice to each bowl and sprinkle in the reserved cilantro leaves and scallions. Finally, float some lemon slices on top and serve immediately.

Fresh Tomato Soup with
Parmesan Croutons and Basil

Serves 4

1½ tablespoons olive oil

1 medium onion, finely chopped

1 medium baking potato, peeled and finely diced

1 lb 8 oz ripe tomatoes, cut in quarters (leave the skin on)

1¼ cups Vegetable Stock (page 128)

Salt and freshly ground black pepper to taste

1 garlic clove, crushed through a press

2 teaspoons chopped fresh basil, plus 4 small sprigs, for serving

2 tablespoons crème fraîche or sour cream, for serving

Parmesan Croutons (page 129), for serving

One of the great treats of summer is the taste of sweet, ripe tomatoes, and this versatile soup, which can be served hot or cold, takes full advantage. In season, almost any kind of flavorful tomato will work here: beefsteak or plum. For brightest flavor, chop the basil just before adding.

1. Gently heat the olive oil in a heavy-bottomed saucepan, then put in the onion and potato and let them cook slowly without browning. This takes 10 to 15 minutes.

2. Now add the tomatoes, stir well, and let them cook for a minute. Pour the stock over the tomatoes, stir, season with salt and pepper, and add the garlic. Cover and allow everything to simmer for 25 minutes.

3. When the soup is ready, let it cool slightly. Then, in batches, purée the soup in a blender or food processor, pouring it into a large bowl. Now return the soup to the saucepan to reheat, taste to check the seasoning, and add the chopped basil. Serve with a swirl of crème fraîche, the croutons, and a sprig of fresh basil. If you wish, cool the soup and refrigerate it until chilled, to serve cold.

Chilled Cucumber Soup
with Yogurt and Mint
Serves 4

1¼ cups plain yogurt

I large seedless (English) cucumber

2 teaspoons chopped fresh mint

⅔ cup sour cream

1 garlic clove, crushed through a press

2 teaspoons fresh lemon juice

A little milk, if needed

Salt and freshly ground black pepper to taste

4 slices of lemon, very thinly sliced, for serving

This cool, light, and subtle soup is incredibly easy and quick to make. However, it does need some fresh summer cucumbers in season for the best flavor of all.

1. First, peel the cucumber with a vegetable peeler, leaving some of the green skin on. Slice the cucumber, reserving a few thin slices to garnish the soup. Place the cucumber in a blender, along with the yogurt, sour cream, and garlic. Blend at the highest speed until the mixture is smooth. Add a seasoning of salt and pepper and the lemon juice. Pour the soup into a tureen and if it seems to be a little too thick, thin it with some cold milk. Now stir in the mint and cover. Refrigerate until very cold, at least several hours.

2. To serve, ladle the soup into individual chilled soup bowls and float a few thin slices of cucumber and a thin slice of lemon on each one.

Fresh Fennel and Tomato Gazpacho
Serves 4

1 lb 8 oz ripe tomatoes

1 largish fennel bulb with fronds (12 oz)

1¼ teaspoons fine salt, preferably sea salt

¾ teaspoon coriander seeds

½ teaspoon mixed peppercorns (black, white, green, and pink)

1 tablespoon extra virgin olive oil

1 small onion, chopped

1 large garlic clove, crushed through a press

1 tablespoon fresh lemon juice

1½ teaspoons balsamic vinegar

¾ teaspoon chopped fresh oregano

1 teaspoon tomato paste

Olive Croutons (page 129), for serving

Almost any type of gazpacho, served ice cold, is one of the nicest first courses in warm weather. This version is quite different from the traditional version on page 40 – much coarser in texture and with the subtle anise flavor of the fennel. Serve warm if it turns chilly, but really cold if presenting chilled. You can even add an ice cube just before serving.

1. First, skin the tomatoes: pour boiling water over them and leave for 1 minute before draining them and slipping off the skins (protect your hands with a cloth if they're too hot). Then chop the tomatoes roughly. Next, trim the green fronds from the fennel (reserve these for the garnish) and cut the bulb into quarters. Trim away the tough core at the base and slice the fennel into thinnish slices. Now place these in a saucepan with the salt and add 2 cups of water. Bring it to a simmer, then cover and simmer gently for 10 minutes.

2. Meanwhile, crush the coriander seeds and mixed peppercorns in a mortar and pestle. Then heat the oil in a large saucepan and add the crushed spices, along with the onion. Let these cook gently for 5 minutes, then add the garlic and cook for another 2 minutes. Now add the chopped tomatoes, lemon juice, vinegar, and oregano, and stir well. Stir in the fennel, along with the water in which it was simmering. Finally, stir in the tomato paste, bring everything to a simmer, and simmer gently, uncovered, for 30 minutes.

3. Let the soup cool a little. In batches, purée the soup in a blender or food processor, and pour it into a large bowl. When the soup has cooled completely, cover the bowl and refrigerate for several hours, until the soup is well chilled. Serve cold, garnished with the olive croutons and the chopped green fennel fronds.

Watercress and Buttermilk Vichyssoise
Serves 6 to 8

8 tablespoons butter

4 medium baking potatoes
(1½ pounds), such as russet or
Burbank, peeled and diced

3 medium leeks, white and pale
green parts only, chopped and
well rinsed

1 medium onion, finely chopped

1 large bunch (12 oz) watercress,
a few leaves reserved for garnish

Salt to taste

7 cups Vegetable Stock (page 128)

1¼ cups buttermilk

Freshly ground black pepper
to taste

This is a very summery, cool soup. The peppery, green watercress leaves are matched perfectly by the soothing acidity of buttermilk. It must be served very cold.

1. First of all, melt the butter in a large saucepan, then add the potatoes, leeks, onion, and half of the watercress. Stir the vegetables around so that they're coated with the melted butter. Next, sprinkle in some salt, cover, and let the vegetables cook over very gentle heat for about 20 minutes, giving the mixture a good stir about halfway through.

2. After that, add the stock, and bring to a simmer. Cover and simmer for 10 to 15 minutes, or until the vegetables are quite tender. Then remove the pan from the heat and let the soup cool a little. Then, in batches, purée the soup in a blender or food processor until smooth, pouring the soup into a large bowl. Let the soup stand until cool.

3. When the soup is cold, stir in three-quarters of the buttermilk and season to taste. Cover the bowl with plastic wrap and refrigerate until the soup is thoroughly chilled – overnight is ideal.

4. When you are ready to serve the soup, put the remaining watercress in a large bowl (don't forget to reserve some leaves for the garnish). Then, using the end of a rolling pin or a pestle, "bruise" the leaves – this will release the oil in the leaves. Now purée the watercress in the blender or food processor with about one-third of the chilled soup. When it is smooth, stir it into the rest of the soup.

5. Serve the soup in bowls that have been very well chilled, and garnish each one with a swirl of the remaining buttermilk and a few reserved watercress leaves.

Summer Pea Soup
Serves 4

4 tablespoons butter

1 (⅛-inch thick) slice pancetta, finely chopped

4 scallions, white and green parts, finely chopped

4 leaves bibb lettuce, finely chopped

1 cup packed fresh baby spinach

2 lb fresh peas, shelled (2 cups shelled peas)

Salt, to taste

1 teaspoon sugar

Freshly ground black pepper to taste

1 tablespoon finely chopped fresh mint

1 to 2 tablespoons crème fraîche

Freshly grated nutmeg

This soup is a lovely dark green color and has all the wonderful ingredients and flavors of peas à la Française – peas, scallions, lettuce, and bacon – blended into a velvety smooth soup.

1. First of all, melt the butter in a large saucepan and gently sauté the pancetta, scallions, lettuce, and spinach for about 5 minutes. Add the peas and some salt, and stir everything together. Then pour in 2¾ cups boiling water. Next, add the sugar, cover, and simmer the peas gently for 10 to 15 minutes, or until they are soft.

2. Let the soup cool a little. In batches, purée the soup in a blender or food processor, pouring the soup into a large bowl. Taste and season with more salt (if it needs it) and pepper, then return to the saucepan and gently reheat it. Stir the mint into the soup and serve in hot bowls, garnishing each one with a spoonful of crème fraîche and a little freshly grated nutmeg just before serving.

Zucchini Soup with Watercress and Pecorino Pesto
Serves 4 to 6

4 tablespoons butter

3 medium zucchini (1 lb), scrubbed but unpeeled, diced

1 small baking potato (4 oz), such as russet or Burbank, peeled and diced

1 large onion, chopped

1 garlic clove, finely chopped

Salt and freshly ground black pepper to taste

3⅓ cups Chicken Stock or Vegetable Stock (page 128)

⅓ cup half-and-half

For the pesto

1 cup packed watercress, including stalks

⅓ cup plus 1 tablespoon extra virgin olive oil

1 tablespoon pine nuts

1 small garlic clove, crushed through a press

¼ cup (1 oz) freshly grated Pecorino Romano or Parmesan cheese

Salt to taste

This light summer soup is perfect for late summer when zucchini are cheap and plentiful. Serve each bowl with a spoonful of the watercress and pecorino pesto zigzagged over the surface of the soup.

1. Begin by melting the butter gently in a large saucepan, add the zucchini, potato, onion, and garlic, and stir everything around so the vegetables are glossy and covered in butter. Add a little salt and pepper, then partially cover the pan and let the vegetables cook gently to release their juices, about 15 minutes. Now add the stock, bring the soup back to a simmer, and cook very gently for 7 to 10 minutes, again partially covered, or until the potatoes are soft and the zucchini are tender.

2. While the soup is simmering, make the pesto. All you do is put the watercress (stalks and all), oil, pine nuts, and garlic, with some salt, in a food processor or blender, and process until you have a smooth purée. Then transfer the purée to a bowl, and stir in the grated cheese.

3. When the soup is ready, let it cool a little. In batches, purée the soup in a blender and transfer it to a large bowl. Next, pour it back into the saucepan, stir in the half-and-half, then gently reheat the soup. Ladle it into bowls. Top each serving with a spoonful of the pesto and, using a skewer or the tip of a small knife, zigzag the pesto all over the surface of the soup. Serve hot.

Autumn

Leek, Onion, and Potato Soup
Serves 4 to 6

4 tablespoons butter

4 large leeks

2 medium baking potatoes, such as russet or Burbank, peeled and diced

1 medium onion, chopped small

3⅓ cups Vegetable Stock (page 128)

1¼ cups milk

salt and freshly ground black pepper to taste

To serve

2 tablespoons heavy cream or crème fraîche, for garnish

1½ tablespoons finely chopped fresh chives or chopped parsley, for garnish

This has proven to be one of the most popular recipes over the years. The chilled version of this soup is a classic vichyssoise. Either way, it's an absolute winner.

1. Begin by trimming the leeks, discarding the tough outer layer. Now split them in half lengthwise. Slice them quite finely, then wash them thoroughly in two or three changes of water, being sure to separate the rings of leeks to remove any hidden grit or dirt. Drain well. In a large, heavy-bottomed saucepan, gently melt the butter, then add the leeks, potatoes, and onion, stirring them all around with a wooden spoon so they get a nice coating of butter. Season with salt and pepper, then cover. Cook the vegetables over very low heat for about 15 minutes.

2. After that, add the stock and milk and bring to a simmer. Cover and simmer very gently for 20 minutes or until the vegetables are soft – if you have the heat too high, the milk in the soup may make it boil over. Now cool the soup a little, then, working in batches, purée it in a blender or food processor, making sure to have a bowl handy to take the puréed soup.

3. Now return the soup to the saucepan and reheat gently, tasting to check the seasoning. Add a swirl of cream or crème fraîche before serving and sprinkle with freshly snipped chives or parsley.

Butternut Squash Soup
with Toasted Corn
Serves 6

2 tablespoons plus 1 teaspoon
butter

1 medium onion, finely chopped

1 lb 8 oz butternut squash
or other winter squash, peeled,
seeds removed, and flesh
chopped into 1-inch dice

4 cups fresh corn kernels
(cut from 5–6 ears)

Salt and freshly ground black
pepper

2½ cups Vegetable Stock
(page 128)

1¼ cups milk

Sweet corn kernels, broiled until golden brown, provide a lovely contrasting garnish to the velvety texture of this creamy soup.

1. Begin by melting 2 tablespoons of the butter in a medium saucepan, then add the onion and cook slowly for about 8 minutes. After that, add the butternut squash, along with 2 cups of the corn. Give everything a good stir and season with salt and pepper. Cover, and keeping the heat low, let the vegetables cook gently and release their juices – this should take about 10 minutes. Next, pour in the stock and milk, and bring to a simmer. Put the lid on, but leave a little gap (so it's not quite on). Cook gently until the vegetables are very tender, about 20 minutes. Keep a close eye on it anyway, since the milk in the soup could make it boil over. (Don't worry if the liquid curdles, because it will smooth out when blended.)

2. While that's happening, preheat the broiler. Melt the remaining 1 teaspoon of butter. Mix the butter with the remaining 2 cups of corn and spread on a rimmed baking sheet. Season with salt and pepper and broil about 3 inches from the heat – it will take about 8 minutes to become nicely toasted and golden, but remember to stir the corn around halfway through so it toasts evenly.

3. When the soup is ready, let it cool a little. Working in batches, purée the soup in a blender or food processor, leaving a little bit of texture – it doesn't need to be absolutely smooth. Have a large bowl handy to pour the puréed soup into. Return the soup to the saucepan and reheat gently. Serve the soup in warm bowls with the toasted corn sprinkled on top.

Saffron Mussel Cream Soup
Serves 4

2 lb 4 oz fresh mussels

2 cups dry white wine

2 good pinches of saffron stamens

4 tablespoons butter

4 shallots, finely chopped

1 large garlic clove, finely chopped

3 tablespoons all-purpose flour

1 cup milk

1 cup crème fraîche or heavy cream

3 tablespoons very finely chopped fresh chives

Salt and freshly ground white pepper to taste

Cultivated mussels, which are much cleaner than wild, have made preparation of this delicate mollusk a snap. White wine and shallots, along with a generous dose of heavy cream and fresh chives, turn the humble shellfish into a very smart soup.

1. Prepare the mussels by discarding any that have broken shells or any that don't close when given a sharp tap with a knife. Then, under cold running water, scrub the mussels, removing any barnacles, and pull out the little hairy beards, if they are present. Place the cleaned mussels in a bowl of clean cold water and swirl them around to get rid of any lingering bits of grit or sand. Drain them into a colander. Next, pour the wine into a large, wide-bottomed saucepan. When the wine comes to the boil, put 2 tablespoons into a small bowl, stir in the saffron, and set aside. Next, add the mussels to the saucepan, cover, and cook on high heat for 4 to 5 minutes. Line a colander with rinsed cheesecloth and place it over a large bowl. When all the mussels have opened, pour them and their liquid into the colander and let them drain. Now rinse out the saucepan (in case there is any fine grit left from the mussels). Melt the butter in it, add the shallots, and cook over low heat until lightly golden, about 5 minutes.

2. Meanwhile, remove the mussels from the shells, discarding the shells as you go, and making sure to throw away any mussels that have not opened during cooking. Now pour the reserved cooking liquid into a bowl. Next, add the garlic to the cooked shallots and cook for 30 seconds. Sprinkle with the flour and, using a small pointed wooden spoon, stir quite vigorously to make a smooth, glossy paste. Now increase the heat to medium and begin to add the reserved mussel cooking liquid, a little at a time, still stirring. When all the liquid has been added, bring the mixture to a simmer and cook on the lowest possible heat for 1 minute, stirring all the time. Next, add the saffron and its soaking liquid, and the milk and crème fraîche. Bring the soup back to a gentle simmer, switch to a balloon whisk, and whisk until you have a smooth, creamy mixture. Now add the shelled mussels and 2 tablespoons of chives, and heat gently for 5 minutes. Season and serve in warmed bowls, garnished with the remaining chopped chives.

Jerusalem Artichoke and Carrot Soup
Serves 6 to 8

1 lb 8 oz Jerusalem artichokes

1 lb carrots

6 tablespoons butter

1 medium onion, coarsely chopped

3 celery ribs, trimmed and chopped

salt and freshly ground black pepper to taste

6 cups Vegetable Stock (page 128)

2–3 tablespoons crème fraîche or sour cream, for garnish

Fresh flat-leaf parsley leaves, for garnish

Jerusalem artichokes, which are actually more closely related to sunflowers than to artichokes, have a pleasingly subtle, nutty taste and crisp texture. Combined with carrots, they make a soup that has an extremely beautiful, rich saffron color.

1. Start by peeling and trimming the artichokes. As you peel them, cut them into rough chunks and place them in a bowl of cold, salted water to prevent them from discoloring. Then peel the carrots and slice them into largish chunks.

2. Now melt the butter in a large saucepan, add the onion and celery, and cook until softened, about 5 minutes, keeping the heat fairly low. Next, drain the artichokes and add them to the pan, along with the carrots. Add some salt and, keeping the heat very low, cover and let the vegetables cook slowly for 10 minutes to release their juices.

3. After that, pour in the stock, stir well, cover again, and simmer, very gently, for 20 minutes, or until the vegetables are soft. Now cool the soup slightly, then purée it in batches in a blender – a large bowl is useful here to put the soup in. Then return the soup to the saucepan, taste to check the seasoning, and reheat very gently until it just comes to a simmer. Serve in hot soup bowls, each garnished with a swirl of crème fraîche and a few parsley leaves.

Black Bean Soup with Black Bean and Tomato Salsa
Serves 4 to 6

1 generous cup dried black beans

2 tablespoons olive oil

3 slices bacon or pancetta, finely chopped

1 large onion, finely chopped

½ cup finely chopped carrot

½ cup pared and finely chopped yellow rutabaga, or another carrot

1 plump garlic clove, crushed through a press

20 sprigs fresh cilantro, leaves and stalks separated, stalks finely chopped and leaves reserved for the salsa

1 teaspoon cumin seeds

4½ cups Chicken Stock (page 128)

1 teaspoon hot red pepper sauce

1 tablespoon fresh lime juice

Salt and freshly ground black pepper to taste

crème fraîche, for garnish

For the salsa

⅓ cup cooked beans from the soup

2 large tomatoes (not too ripe), skinned (see page 18)

1 small red onion, finely chopped

1 green chili, such as jalapeño, seeded and chopped

3 tablespoons chopped fresh cilantro leaves

1 tablespoon extra virgin olive oil

1 tablespoon fresh lime juice

salt and freshly ground black pepper to taste

This soup is stunning and one you'll want to make over and over again. If you forget to soak the beans overnight, bring them up to the boil for 10 minutes, then presoak them for two hours. If you're entertaining and want to have some fun, serve this soup, half and half, with Tuscan White Bean Soup (see picture opposite and page 81).

1. Start the soup the night before by placing the beans into a large bowl and adding enough cold water to cover by 2 inches. The next day, drain them in a colander and rinse them under cold water. Now heat the olive oil in a large saucepan. As soon as it's really hot, add the chopped bacon and cook for about 5 minutes, until crisp. Then turn the heat down to medium, stir in the onion, carrot, rutabaga (if using), garlic, and cilantro stalks. Cook, covered, for 10 minutes, stirring everything around once or twice.

2. While that's happening, heat a small skillet pan over medium heat, then add the cumin seeds and dry-roast them for about 1 minute until they become aromatic and start to dance in the pan. Now crush them into a coarse powder with a mortar and pestle. Add them to the vegetables, along with the drained beans, stock, and hot pepper sauce (but no salt at this stage). Bring to a gentle simmer and cook, covered, for about 1½ hours, until the beans are tender. When the time is up, use a slotted spoon to remove ⅓ cup of the beans, rinse and drain them in a sieve, and reserve them for the salsa. Now let the soup cool a little, then purée it in batches in a blender or food processor with a bowl to hand to put the puréed soup in. Now return the soup to the saucepan, add the lime juice, season with salt and pepper, and it's ready for reheating.

3. To make the salsa, cut the skinned tomatoes in half and gently squeeze each half in your hand to remove the seeds, then chop the tomato into small dice and place it in a bowl, along with the reserved beans, the red onion, chili, cilantro leaves, and the olive oil. Then add the lime juice and some salt and pepper, and set aside for the flavors to mingle for about 1 hour. To serve the soup, reheat it gently, being careful not to allow it to come to the boil, because this will spoil the flavor of the soup. Serve in warm soup bowls, adding a spoonful of crème fraîche and sprinkling a spoonful of salsa on top.

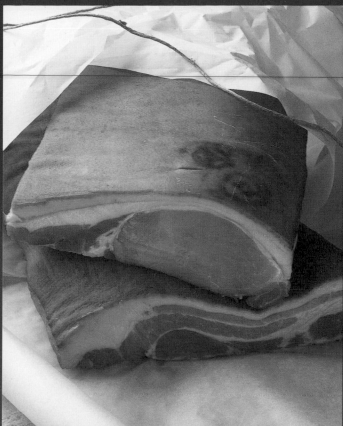

Wild Mushroom and Walnut Soup
Serves 8

1 oz dried porcini mushrooms

4 tablespoons butter

4 oz cremini mushrooms, chopped

2 medium carrots, chopped

2 celery ribs, chopped

1 medium onion, chopped

1 leek, white and pale green part chopped and well rinsed (see page 8)

1 teaspoon chopped fresh thyme

½ teaspoon chopped fresh sage

2 garlic cloves, crushed through a press

2 bay leaves

salt to taste

To finish

2 tablespoons butter

8 oz cremini mushrooms, 4 small ones reserved for garnish, and the remainder finely chopped

1 cup walnuts (4 oz), ground in a nut mill or food processor

salt and freshly ground black pepper to taste

⅓ cup half-and-half, plus a little more for garnish

⅓ cup dry sherry

2 teaspoons fresh lemon juice

A mixture of dried porcini and fresh white mushrooms, combined with walnuts and aromatics and spiked with sherry, creates an unusual and special soup appropriate for a dinner party or luncheon.

1. First, place the dried mushrooms in a small bowl with 1¼ cups boiling water and set aside to soak for 30 minutes. Meanwhile, in a very large saucepan melt the 4 tablespoons of butter, then add the 4 oz chopped cremini mushrooms, the carrots, celery, onion, leek, thyme, sage, garlic, and bay leaves. Stir well over low heat until everything is glistening with a coating of butter. Place a wire sieve lined with moistened paper towels over a bowl. Drain the soaked mushroom, reserving the soaking liquid. Add the soaked mushrooms and their soaking liquid and 2 quarts hot water to the saucepan. Add some salt, then bring to a gentle simmer and, keeping the heat low, let the soup barely simmer for 1 hour.

2. After that, place a colander over a large bowl and strain the soup into it. Remove the bay leaves, and, in batches, purée the vegetables with a little bit of the cooking liquid in a blender or food processor, pouring the purée into a large bowl. Add the remaining cooking liquid and whisk until well combined.

3. To finish the soup, return saucepan to low heat, add the 2 tablespoons butter, and melt it. Add the 8 oz mushrooms and lightly sauté them for about 5 minutes. After that, pour in the soup mixture, stir in the ground walnuts, season with salt and pepper, and let it continue cooking gently for 10 minutes. While that's happening, use your sharpest knife to slice the 4 whole mushrooms into wafer-thin slices for a garnish. When you are ready to serve the soup, stir in the half-and-half, sherry, and lemon juice. Serve piping hot with a swirl of cream and the slices of raw mushroom floating on top.

Cauliflower Soup with Roquefort Cheese
Serves 4 to 6

1 good-sized cauliflower
(about 1 lb 4 oz)

2 bay leaves

salt to taste

2 tablespoons butter

1 medium onion, chopped

2 sticks celery, chopped

1 large leek, white and pale green
parts chopped and rinsed
(see page 8)

1 small baking potato (4 oz), such
as russet or Burbank, peeled and
diced

½ cup crumbled Roquefort cheese
(2 oz)

2 tablespoons crème fraîche or
heavy cream

freshly ground black pepper to
taste

a little more crème fraîche or
heavy cream, for garnish (optional)

1 tablespoon finely chopped fresh
chives, for garnish

Pungent Roquefort adds just the right amount of interest to the pleasing blandness of cauliflower, but another blue cheese or an aged Cheddar could be used.

1. The stock for this is very simply made with all the cauliflower trimmings. Trim the cauliflower into small florets and set them aside. Place the trimmings, along with any green stems, in a medium saucepan. Then add 6 cups of water, the bay leaves, and some salt, and bring it to a boil. Cover and simmer for 20 minutes.

2. Meanwhile, take another large saucepan with a well-fitting lid, melt the butter in it over low heat, then add the onion, celery, leek, and potato. Cover and let the vegetables cook gently for 15 minutes. When the stock is ready, strain it into the pan to join the vegetables, adding the bay leaves as well but throwing out the solids. Now add the cauliflower florets and return the soup to a simmer. Cook very gently, uncovered, for 20 to 25 minutes, or until the cauliflower is completely tender.

3. Next, remove the bay leaves and let the soup cool a little. In batches, purée the soup in a blender or food processor, pouring the puréed soup into a bowl. Return the soup to the saucepan, stir in the Roquefort and crème fraîche, stirring until the cheese has melted and the soup is hot but not boiling. Check the seasoning for salt and pepper. Serve in hot bowls, garnished with a little more crème fraîche if you like, and the chives.

Tomato, Apple, and Celery Cream Soup
Serves 4

4 tablespoons butter

1 small onion (4 oz), finely chopped

1 medium tomato (6 oz), quartered, including stalk, if attached

1 small Granny Smith apple (6 oz), quartered and peeled

3 medium celery ribs (6 oz), cut into 2 inch lengths, including leaves

¼ cup dry sherry

freshly grated nutmeg

1 small pinch of ground ginger

¼ teaspoon salt

freshly ground black pepper to taste

2¼ cups Chicken Stock or Vegetable Stock (page 128)

apple slices and snipped fresh chives, for garnish

Croutons (page 129), for serving

Slowly cooking the vegetables and apple before adding the stock intensifies the flavors here in this delicate, slightly sweet soup. Weights for the main ingredients are included, since the proportions will make a difference in the final result. If you don't have a kitchen scale, weigh them at the market and take note.

1. First, melt the butter in a large, heavy saucepan, then add the onion and cook gently until golden, about 10 minutes, stirring often so that it doesn't burn or stick to the bottom. Add the tomato, apple, celery, sherry, nutmeg, ginger, salt, and pepper to the saucepan. Cut two double-thick rounds of waxed paper to fit inside of the saucepan. Dampen them well with cold water, place them over the ingredients, and cover.

2. Simmer very gently for 1 hour, stirring from time to time to check that nothing is sticking. After that, remove the paper and stir in the stock. Now slightly cool the soup and transfer it – in batches – to a blender or food processor to purée it. Rub the soup through a sieve to remove seeds and stalks, and return the soup to a clean saucepan. Reheat, check the seasoning, ladle into warmed soup bowls, and garnish each serving with an apple slice and some snipped chives. Serve with the croutons.

Tuscan White Bean Soup with Crispy Shallots and Pancetta
Serves 4

1 cup dried cannellini (white kidney) beans

4 tablespoons extra virgin olive oil

1 large onion, chopped

2 plump garlic cloves, crushed under a knife and peeled

1 celery rib, chopped

1 large sprig each of fresh parsley, thyme, and rosemary, leaves only

1 bay leaf

freshly ground black pepper to taste

4¾ cups Chicken Stock (page 128)

Juice of ½ lemon

Salt to taste

For the crsipy shallots and pancetta garnish

3 tablespoons extra virgin olive oil

4 shallots, finely sliced into rings

3 oz thinly sliced pancetta or bacon

Cannellini are amazingly versatile – great used whole in salads, mashed into dips, and, as here, simmered and then pureed into soup. The beans soak up seasonings they are cooked with, which include good olive oil, garlic, and a touch of lemon. The garnish of fried shallots and pancetta, or bacon, also add a nice hit of flavor.

1. First of all, soak the beans in a large bowl with enough cold water to cover by 2 inches overnight. Or put them in a saucepan with the same amount of cold water, bring to a boil, cook for 10 minutes, remove from the heat, and set aside for 2 hours.

2. When you're ready to make the soup, heat 2 tablespoons of the olive oil in a large saucepan, and gently cook the onion in it for 5 minutes. Then add the garlic and continue to cook gently for about 1 minute. After that, add the drained beans, celery, parsley, thyme, rosemary, bay leaf, and black pepper, but no salt at this stage. Now pour in the stock and stir well. As soon as it comes to a gentle simmer, cover, and keep it at the gentlest simmer for 1½ hours, stirring it from time to time. When the time is up, check if the beans are tender and, if not, cook them for another 15 to 30 minutes. When the beans are tender, season with salt, let cool a little, then purée them in a blender in batches (pour the puréed soup into a large bowl). When you are ready to serve the soup, reheat it gently without letting it come to the boil, then add the lemon juice, check the seasoning, and add the remaining 2 tablespoons of olive oil just before serving.

3. While the soup reheats, make the garnish: cut the pancetta into fine shreds with a sharp knife, and separate the shreds. Now heat 2 tablespoons of the oil in a large skillet over high heat. When it is hot and shimmering, add the shallots and fry for 3 to 4 minutes, stirring occasionally so they don't stick to the skillet. When they are crisp and golden brown, use a slotted spoon and transfer them to crumpled paper towels to drain. Now heat the remaining 1 tablespoon of oil in the same skillet and fry the pancetta strips over high heat for about 2 minutes until they, too, are golden and crunchy. Drain on paper towels, then sprinkle the shallots and pancetta on the soup as it goes to the table.

North African Lamb Soup with Chickpeas and Couscous
Serves 6

⅔ cup dried chickpeas (garbanzo beans)

1¼ teaspoons coriander seeds

1¼ teaspoons cumin seeds

2 tablespoons peanut or other flavorless oil

1 large onion, chopped

2 garlic cloves, crushed through a press and mixed with with 1 teaspoon coarse salt

1¼ teaspoons ground allspice

2½ teaspoons chili powder

6 oz trimmed boneless leg of lamb, finely chopped with a sharp knife

⅓ cup tomato paste

1 fresh green chili, seeded and chopped

2 teaspoons sugar

2½ cups lamb stock (see above)

⅓ cup couscous

1 tablespoon chopped fresh parsley

1 tablespoon chopped fresh mint

Salt, to taste

Lemon wedges, for serving

Pita bread, for serving

A cross between a soup and a stew, this hearty meal-in-a bowl is irresistibly spiced and so good you'll make it again and again. For lamb stock, make the Beef Stock on page 128, and substitute chunks of lamb neck for the beef bones.

1. First you need to place the chickpeas in a bowl, add enough cold water to cover them by 2 inches, and let them stand overnight.

2. To make the soup, preheat a small skillet over medium heat. Add the coriander and cumin seeds and dry-roast them for about 2 to 3 minutes, moving them around the pan until they change color and begin to dance. This will draw out their full spicy flavor. Now crush them quite finely with a mortar and pestle.

3. Next, heat 1 tablespoon of the oil in a large saucepan and gently cook the onion until soft and lightly browned, about 5 or 6 minutes. Add the garlic paste and let that cook for another 2 minutes. After that, add the crushed seeds, the allspice, and chili powder, and stir them into the juices in the pan. Now transfer all this to a plate and set aside. Heat the remaining 1 tablespoon of oil in the saucepan until it's very hot. Then add the lamb and brown it, turning the pieces often to keep them on the move.

4. Turn the heat down and return the onion and spice mixture to the pan to join the meat, adding the tomato paste, green chili, and sugar. Stir everything together, then add the stock and 3⅓ cups water. Give it another good stir, then drain the soaked chickpeas, discarding their soaking liquid, and add them to the pan. Give a final stir, cover, and simmer as gently as possible for 1 hour, or until the chickpeas are tender.

5. When you're ready to serve the soup, taste it, add some salt, then stir in the couscous, parsley, and mint and remove the pan from the heat. Cover and set aside for 3 minutes. Serve in hot soup bowls with lemon wedges to squeeze into the soup and some warm pita bread.

Vegetable Mulligatawny
Serves 8

8 tablespoons butter

3 large onions, chopped

3 whole cardamom pods, seeds only

1½ teaspoons coriander seeds

1 teaspoon cumin seeds

1 teaspoon fennel seeds

4 large zucchini (1½ pounds), cut into 1-inch cubes

1 large baking potato, such as russet or Burbank, peeled and cut into 1-inch cubes

1 ripe large tomato, skinned and chopped (see page 18)

3⅓ cups Vegetable Stock (page 128), heated

⅓ cup basmati rice

Croutons (page 129), for serving

Salt and freshly ground black pepper to taste

Indian spices and basmati rice turn common vegetables into an uncommonly good soup, perfect for a chilly autumn day. Add some whole-grain bread and excellent cheese, and you have the perfect vegetarian lunch.

1. First, melt the butter in a large saucepan over medium-low heat. Add the onions and cook until they're a golden brown color, about 10 minutes. Now place the cardamom, coriander, cumin, and fennel seeds in a small skillet to dry-roast over medium heat – this will take 2 to 3 minutes. As soon as the seeds start to jump in the skillet, crush them finely in a mortar and pestle, then add them to the onions.

2. Now add the zucchini, potato, and tomatoes to the saucepan. Season well, then cover and let the vegetables cook gently in their own juices until soft, about 20 minutes.

3. While the vegetables are cooking, bring ¾ cup water to a boil in a small saucepan. Add the rice and cover. Reduce the heat to the lowest setting and simmer until the rice is tender, about 15 minutes. Remove from the heat.

4. Next, when the vegetables have cooled a little, purée them in batches in a blender or food processor, putting each batch in a large bowl. Then pour the purée back into the saucepan and stir in the cooked rice, together with the hot stock. Reheat gently and cook for about 5 minutes more. Serve with some crisp croutons sprinkled in each bowl.

Spiced Parsnip and Apple Soup with Parsnip Chips
Serves 6

1¼ teaspoons coriander seeds

1¼ teaspoons cumin seeds

6 whole cardamom pods, seeds only

3 tablespoons butter

1 tablespoon peanut or other flavorless oil

2 medium onions, chopped

2 garlic cloves, chopped

1¼ teaspoons ground turmeric

1¼ teaspoons ground ginger

1 lb 8 oz parsnips

5 cups Vegetable Stock or Chicken Stock (page 128)

Salt and freshly ground black pepper to taste

Parsnip Chips (page 130)

1 Granny Smith apple, for serving

To those who love them, parsnips are an incredibly seductive root vegetable. Here they play off the sweetness of apple and the zip of ground ginger and cardamom to make a lovely soup that's sure to attract attention.

1. Begin by heating a small skillet and dry-roasting the coriander, cumin, and cardamom seeds – this is to toast them and draw out their flavor. After 2 to 3 minutes they will change color and start to jump in the pan. Remove them from the pan and crush them finely with a mortar and pestle.

2. Next, heat the butter and oil in a large saucepan until the butter begins to foam, then add the onions and gently cook for about 5 minutes. Add the garlic and let it cook for another 2 minutes. Add the toasted spices, along with the turmeric and ginger. Now stir and let it continue to cook gently for a few more minutes. Meanwhile, peel and chop the parsnips into 1-inch dice. Add the parsnips to the saucepan, stirring well, then pour in the stock, add some salt and pepper, and let the soup simmer, uncovered, as gently as possible for 1 hour, until the parsnips are very tender.

3. When the soup has been simmering for an hour, remove it from the heat and cool it slightly. Purée the soup in batches in a blender or food processor, then pour the soup into a bowl. Now return it to the saucepan, taste to check the seasoning, then when you're ready to serve, reheat very gently. While that's happening, peel the apple and as the soup just reaches a simmer, grate the apple into it. Be careful to let the soup barely simmer for only 3 to 4 minutes. Serve in hot soup bowls, garnished with the parsnip chips.

Roasted Pumpkin Soup with Melting Cheese
Serves 6

3-3 lb 8 oz cooking pumpkin, such as pie, cheese, or sugar pumpkin

1 tablespoon peanut or other flavorless oil

2 tablespoons butter

1 large onion, finely chopped

3⅓ cups Vegetable Stock or Chicken Stock (page 128)

1¾ cups whole milk

Freshly grated nutmeg

Salt and freshly ground black pepper to taste

To serve

6 oz Gruyère or Italian Fontina cheese, 4 oz cut into ¼-inch dice (1 cup), and 2 oz coarsely shredded (½ cup)

2 tablespoons crème fraîche or heavy cream, for garnish

Croutons (page 129), optional

Chopped fresh flat-leaf parsley, for garnish

After roasting to concentrate its flavor, pumpkin cooks up to a really velvety soup. Just before serving, tiny cubes of two kinds of quick-melting cheese are added, along with croutons for texture.

1. Begin by preheating the oven to 450°F. Cut the pumpkin in half through the stalk, then cut each half into quarters. Scoop out the seeds, using a large spoon. Then brush the surface of each section with the oil. Place the pumpkin pieces on a heavy baking sheet. Season with salt and pepper. Bake in the upper third of the oven and roast for 25 to 30 minutes or until tender when pierced with a skewer.

2. Meanwhile, melt the butter in a large saucepan over a high heat, add the onion, stir it around, and when it begins to color around the edges, after about 5 minutes, turn the heat down. Let it cook very gently, uncovered, giving it a stir from time to time, for about 20 minutes, until deep golden brown.

3. Remove the pumpkin from the oven and let it cool until easy to handle. Now add the stock and the milk to the saucepan, and slowly bring the mixture up to a simmer. Next, scoop out the flesh of the pumpkin with a sharp knife and add it to the saucepan, together with a seasoning of salt, pepper, and nutmeg. Then let it all simmer very gently for about 15 to 20 minutes.

4. Next, cool the soup a little. In batches, purée it in a blender or food processor, and transfer the puréed soup to a large bowl. It's best to pass it through a wire sieve as well, in case there are any unblended fibrous bits. Taste and season well. When you're ready to serve the soup, reheat it gently in the saucepan just up to a simmer, being careful not to let it boil.

5. Finally, stir in the diced cheese, then ladle the soup into warm soup bowls. Garnish each bowl with a spoonful of crème fraîche and scatter with the grated cheese, a few croutons as well if you like them, and a sprinkling of parsley.

Slow-Cooked Celery and Celery Root Soup
Serves 6

6 large celery ribs (1 lb), with a few leaves reserved for garnish

1 large or 2 medium (1 lb 4 oz) celery root

1 medium onion

6 cups Vegetable Stock (page 128), heated

3 bay leaves

Salt and freshly ground black pepper to taste

To serve

2 tablespoons plain yogurt or crème fraîche, for serving

2 teaspoons celery salt, for garnish

Celery root, or celeriac, is a variety of celery grown for its gnarly, but delicious, root. It has a strong, almost nutty flavor that is reminiscent of, although not at all the same as, the kind of celery we are used to munching on, and is probably most famous for its use in celery root remoulade. Here the two cousins are combined in a nonfat soup.

1. Preheat the oven to 275°F. Just a word first about preparing the vegetables. The large, outer celery ribs are fine for soups, but remove the strings with a vegetable peeler first. Save the tender celery hearts for munching as a healthy snack. When paring the celery root with a sharp knife (a peeler doesn't always work here), you may lose quite a bit of the outside, because it's very fibrous, which is why I suggest buying a bit more than you will need for the soup. Do not try to peel the gnarly bits; just cut them off. You should end up with about 1 pound. You want equal amounts of celery and celery root by weight, so use kitchen scale if you have one. Cut the celery and celery root, as well as the onion, into large chunks.

2. Pop the vegetables into a medium flameproof casserole with a lid. Then add the hot stock and bay leaves, along with some salt and pepper. Bring it all up to a simmer on the stove, then cover the casserole and transfer it to the oven. Simmer very gently and slowly for 3 hours. Remove the bay leaves, allow the soup to cool a little, then blend in batches until smooth. A large bowl to put each batch in is helpful here.

3. Return the soup to the casserole and bring it back to a gentle simmer, tasting to check the seasoning before serving. Serve in hot bowls with the yogurt or crème fraîche spooned on top, garnished with a sprinkle of celery salt and perhaps a few celery leaves.

Winter

Cream of Celery Soup
Serves 4

2 tablespoons butter

6 medium celery ribs, chopped, leaves reserved

1 small baking potato, such as russet or Burbank, peeled and diced

2 medium leeks, white parts only, sliced and washed

2¼ cups Vegetable Stock or Chicken Stock (page 128)

1¼ cups milk

¼ teaspoon celery seeds

Salt to taste

2 tablespoons heavy cream or crème fraîche

A good grating of fresh nutmeg

Freshly ground black pepper to taste

No, this nothing like the kind you ate out of a can when you where little. It's a light, subtle soup, seasoned only with celery seed and nutmeg. While you may not think of celery as a seasonal vegetable, it is sweetest after there has been a light frost.

1. In a large saucepan, melt the butter over low heat. Then add the celery with the potatoes and leeks. Stir to coat the vegetables with butter, cover, and cook very gently for about 15 minutes, shaking the pan from time to time to prevent the vegetables from sticking.

2. Next, pour in the stock and milk and sprinkle in the celery seeds and some salt. Bring the soup to a simmer, cover again, and cook over very low heat for 20 to 25 minutes or until the vegetables are really tender. Let the soup cool a little. In batches, purée the soup in a blender or food processor, pouring the soup into a large bowl. Return the soup to the saucepan and add the cream and nutmeg. Bring the soup back to the boil, check the seasoning, adding salt and pepper if necessary. Just before serving, chop the reserved celery leaves and stir them into the soup to give it extra color.

Chestnut Soup with Bacon and Thyme Croutons
Serves 4

7 ounces vacuum-packed cooked chestnuts

1 celery rib, chopped

1 small onion, chopped

1 small carrot, chopped

4½ cups Ham Stock or Vegetable Stock (page 128)

Salt and freshly ground black pepper to taste

For the croutons

4 tablespoons olive oil

1 slice bacon, very finely chopped

4 slices firm, stale white bread, cut into small cubes

½ teaspoon finely chopped fresh thyme leaves

A bone from a baked ham (or even smoked ham hocks) makes a good stock for this excellent soup, but even if you use simple vegetable broth, you'll love the results. To save time and effort, buy vacuum-packed chestnuts that are already cooked and peeled.

1. To make the soup, you simply place chestnuts, celery, onion, and carrot in a large saucepan, stir in the stock, season lightly with salt and pepper, and bring to a simmer. Cover and simmer very gently for 45 minutes.

2. While that's happening, you can prepare the croutons. Heat the oil in a large frying pan and cook the bacon gently for 5 minutes. Then turn the heat up to its highest setting, add the bread cubes together with the thyme, and toss them around (keeping them constantly on the move) until the croutons and bacon have turned a deep golden brown color and become very crisp and crunchy. Using a slotted spoon, transfer them to paper towels to drain and cool.

3. As soon as the soup is ready, let it cool slightly. In batches, purée the soup in a blender or food processor, and pour it into a large bowl. Reheat the soup in the saucepan, season to taste, and serve in warmed soup bowls, with the croutons, bacon, and thyme sprinkled over.

Farmhouse Vegetable Soup with Bacon, Beans, and Sausage
Serves 8

2 lb ham hocks, or bacon

¾ cup dried cannellini (white kidney) beans, generously covered with cold water and soaked overnight

A few parsley stalks

A sprig of thyme

4 Italian pork sausages

2 tablespoons peanut or other flavorless oil

1 plump garlic clove, crushed through a press

2 medium leeks, white parts only, cut into ¼-inch thick rings, well washed

1 small onion, chopped

2 medium carrots, cut into ¼-inch rounds

1 small turnip, peeled and cut into ½-inch chunks

1 celery rib, chopped

2 small all-purpose potatoes, peeled and cut into ½-inch dice

3 cups finely shredded Savoy cabbage

Salt and freshly ground black pepper to taste

Chopped fresh parsley, for garnish

Extra virgin olive oil, for serving

La Potée, as this country French dish is called, makes a hearty meal all by itself. Serve with thick slices of grilled peasant or sourdough bread brushed with fruity olive oil.

1. Place the ham hocks in a medium saucepan and cover with cold water. Bring to a simmer and cook over medium heat for 10 minutes. Drain, discarding the liquid, and rinse under cold water. (This will reduce the smoke flavor in the ham.)

2. Drain the beans and reserve the soaking liquid. Measure and add enough cold water to make 9 cups. Place the ham hocks, beans, soaking liquid, parsley, and thyme in a large soup pot (at least 6 quarts) and bring to a boil. Cook for 10 minutes, skimming off any scum as it appears. Cover and simmer until the meat is falling from the ham hock bones, about 1½ hours. Meanwhile, in a skillet, slowly brown the sausages in a tablespoon of the oil. When they're a nice brown color all over, transfer them to a plate and slice into ¼ inch-thick rounds.

3. Next, when the hocks are ready, lift them from the pot and onto a board. Then drain the rest of the ingredients from the pan in a colander, set over a large bowl, reserving the cooking liquid and beans but discarding the parsley and thyme stalks. Rinse out the pot and add the remaining tablespoon of oil to it. Heat the oil and stir in the garlic, then the leeks, onion, carrots, turnip, celery, and potatoes. Cover and cook gently for about 15 minutes or until the vegetables are tender. Meanwhile, skin the ham hocks, remove all the excess fat, and chop the meat into smallish, soup-size pieces. When the vegetables are ready, return the pieces of ham, along with the beans, to the saucepan. Add enough of the cooking liquid to give the whole thing a suitably soupy consistency – about 6 cups – and season with plenty of pepper. Bring the soup back to a boil, then add the sliced sausage and cabbage. Simmer for another few minutes, uncovered, or until the cabbage has wilted. Ladle the piping hot soup into deep bowls and garnish each one with a scattering of chopped parsley and a drizzle of extra virgin olive oil.

Jerusalem Artichoke and Leek Soup
Serves 6

1 lb Jerusalem artichokes

2 large leeks

1 small onion

6 cups Vegetable Stock
(page 128), heated

3 bay leaves

Salt and freshly ground black
pepper to taste

2 tablespoons natural yogurt,
for serving

Freshly snipped chives,
for garnish

This soup is extremely low in fat and has a lovely pure vegetable flavor because it's given a long, slow treatment. Serve it with a swirl of natural yogurt and, if you like, a few snipped chives.

1. Start by peeling and cutting off the knobs from the artichokes. As you peel them, cut them into rough chunks and toss them into a bowl of cold salted water to prevent any discoloring. Now prepare the leeks. First, trim the tough green tops and throw them out, then make a vertical split about halfway down the center of each leek and clean them by running them under cold water tap you fan out the layers – this will rid them of any hidden dust and grit. Then slice them in half lengthways and chop into large chunks, and after that, peel the onion and cut that into large chunks, too.

2. Preheat the oven to 275°F. All you do now is toss the artichokes, leeks, and onion into a large flameproof casserole with a cover. Then add the stock and bay leaves, along with some salt and pepper. Bring the soup to a simmer on the stove. Cover and transfer to the oven. Simmer very gently and slowly until the artichokes are very tender, for 3 hours.

3. When the time is up, remove the bay leaves and allow the soup to cool a little. In batches, purée the soup in a blender or food processor, pouring the puréed soup into a large bowl. Return the soup to the casserole and bring it back to a gentle simmer, tasting to check the seasoning before serving. Serve in hot bowls with the yogurt swirled in and a few chives sprinkled on top.

French Onion Soup
Serves 6

For the croutons

1 tablespoon olive oil

1–2 garlic cloves, crushed through a press

1 baguette, cut on the diagonal into six 1 inch-thick slices

For the soup

4 tablespoons butter

2 tablespoons olive oil

1 lb 8 oz onions, thinly sliced

2 garlic cloves, finely chopped

½ teaspoon sugar

5 cups Beef Stock (page 128)

1¼ cups dry white wine

Salt and freshly ground black pepper to taste

2 tablespoons Cognac (optional)

2 cups (8 oz) shredded Gruyère cheese

There are few things more comforting than making a real French Onion Soup – slowly cooked, caramelized onions that turn mellow and sweet in a broth laced with white wine and Cognac. The whole thing is finished off with crunchy baked croutons of crusty bread topped with melted, toasted cheese.

1. First make the croutons. Preheat the oven to 350°F. Now drizzle the olive oil onto a large, heavy baking sheet and add the crushed garlic. Then, using your hands, spread the oil and garlic all over the sheet. Now place the bread on top of the oil and turn over each one so that both sides have been lightly coated with the oil. Bake them for 20 to 25 minutes until the croutons are crisp and crunchy. Remove from the oven and set aside to cool.

2. Next, place a large, heavy-bottomed saucepan or flameproof casserole over high heat and melt the oil and butter together. When this is very hot, add the onions, garlic, and sugar. Keep stirring them from time to time until the edges of the onions have turned dark – this will take about 6 minutes. Then reduce the heat to its lowest setting and leave the onions to keep cooking very slowly for about 30 minutes, by which time the base of the saucepan will be covered with a rich, nut-brown, caramelized film. After that, pour in the stock and white wine, season, and stir with a wooden spoon, scraping the base of the pan well. As soon as it comes to a simmer, turn down the heat to its lowest setting. Cook the soup very gently, uncovered, for about 1 hour.

3. All this can be done in advance, but when you're ready to serve the soup, bring it back up to a simmer, taste to check for seasoning – and if it's extra-cold outside, add a couple of tablespoons of Cognac. Warm a flameproof tureen or crocks in a preheated 200°F oven and preheat the broiler to its highest setting. Then ladle in the hot soup and top with the croutons, allowing them to float on the top of the soup.

4. Now sprinkle the grated Gruyère thickly over the croutons and place the tureen or crocks under the broiler until the cheese is golden brown and bubbling. Serve immediately – and don't forget to warn your guests that everything is very hot!

Bean, Bacon, and Parsley Soup
Serves 4

1 cup dried lima beans

2 tablespoons peanut or other flavorless oil

4 slices bacon, chopped

1 bay leaf

2 tablespoons butter

1 medium onion, finely chopped

1 medium leek, white and pale green part only, finely chopped and well rinsed

2 small celery ribs, finely chopped

1 large garlic clove, crushed through a press

About ⅔ cup milk

Salt and freshly ground black pepper to taste

3 tablespoons chopped fresh parsley

After being soaked and cooked, fat lima beans plump up to make a good, thick, creamy soup. They also have the great virtue of being able to absorb other flavors really well.

1. First of all, you need to soak the beans overnight in a large saucepan with enough cold water to cover them by 2 inches. Or, using the same amount of cold water, bring them to a boil and boil for 10 minutes, then let them soak for 2 hours. Either way, drain the beans.

2. Now heat 1 tablespoon of the oil in a medium skillet and cook the bacon in it for 5 minutes or until lightly crispy and golden. Remove the bacon from the pan with a draining spoon and set aside.

3. Next, combine the drained beans, 1 quart water, and the bay leaf in a pot. Bring to the boil and partially cover. Simmer gently for 20 to 30 minutes or until the beans are tender, skimming off any scum that appears on the surface.

4. Meanwhile, heat the butter and remaining 3 tablespoons of the oil in a large saucepan. Add the chopped onion, leek, and celery. Stir to coat everything with butter and oil, and cook over low heat for about 10 minutes.

5. Now add the bacon, and the cooked beans and their cooking liquor to the vegetables, discarding the bay leaf. Next, add the garlic and cover. Simmer for 10 minutes, or until the beans and vegetables are soft. Mash the beans against the sides of the pan with a large fork to thicken the soup. Now add milk, season with salt and a generous grinding of black pepper, and stir everything together. Add the chopped parsley and serve.

Lentil Soup with Bacon and Cabbage
Serves 4 to 6

1 tablespoon peanut or other flavorless oil

4 slices bacon or pancetta, finely chopped

2 medium onions, finely chopped

2 medium carrots, finely chopped

2 celery ribs, thinly sliced

1 scant cup (6 oz) lentils, preferably Puy lentils

1 cup canned plum tomatoes

2 garlic cloves, crushed through a press

7 cups Vegetable Stock (page 128)

3 cups finely shredded Savoy cabbage

Salt and freshly ground black pepper to taste

2 tablespoons chopped fresh parsley

This is a very substantial soup, best made with the tiny French, greeny-black Puy lentils. If you can't get these, use green-brown lentils, which don't have the depth of flavor of the Puy lentils but are still excellent and can be used in the same way.

1. Heat the oil in a large saucepan and cook the bacon in it until the fat begins to melt. Then stir in the onions, carrots, and celery, and with the heat fairly high, toss them around in the pan. Cook, stirring now and then, until the vegetables are a little brown around the edges, about 6 minutes.

2. Next, stir in the lentils, plus the tomatoes, followed by the garlic. Stir everything together, and pour in the stock. As soon as the soup comes to the boil, cover and simmer, as gently as possible, until the lentils are tender, about 30 minutes. Then add the cabbage and cook for 5 minutes or until the cabbage has wilted. Taste and season with salt and plenty of pepper. Just before serving, stir in the chopped parsley.

Malaysian Seafood Soup with Coconut Milk, Basil, and Mint
Serves 4

24 large shrimp

24 fresh mussels

4 oz medium-thick dried white rice noodles

4 shallots, peeled

2 lemon grass stalks, trimmed and outer layer removed, tender bulb chopped

3 medium fresh red chilies, such as Thai or serrano, deseeded and chopped

One ¼-inch thick slice fresh galangal or root ginger, peeled and roughly chopped

1¼ teaspoons dried shrimp paste

1¼ teaspoons ground turmeric

½ cup unsalted macadamia nuts or peanuts

1 tablespoon peanut or other flavorless oil

1¾ cups canned coconut milk

¼ cucumber, peeled

2 cups bean sprouts

Juice of 1 lime

10 basil leaves, roughly shredded

20 mint leaves, roughly shredded

Salt, preferably sea salt, to taste

A rich, spicy stew of shrimp, mussels, and rice noodles, swimming in a savory, highly seasoned broth, this exotic dish is a main-course soup guaranteed to delight anyone who loves spices.

1. First of all, you need to prepare the seafood. Peel the shrimp, then run the point of a small, sharp knife along the back of each one and remove any black threads that may be present. Now scrub the mussels under cold running water, remove any barnacles, and pull off the little hairy beards, if present. Discard any mussels that are broken or don't close when given a sharp tap with a knife.

2. Now place the rice noodles in a bowl and cover with boiling water, then let stand for 10 minutes – they won't need any further cooking, just reheating. Drain the noodles in a colander, rinse them in cold water, and set aside.

3. Next, process the shallots, lemon grass, chilies, galangal, shrimp paste, and turmeric, plus 1 tablespoon of water, in a blender or the bowl of a food processor and blend until smooth; set the paste aside. Place the macadamias in a medium saucepan and dry-roast over medium heat until golden brown, transfer to a plate, and set aside. Add the oil to the same saucepan and, when warm, add the prepared paste and stir over medium heat for 2 minutes. Stir in the coconut milk and simmer gently for 10 minutes.

4. Meanwhile, cut the cucumber into four slices lengthwise, then cut each into four long strips. Next, roughly chop the cooled nuts. When the coconut-milk mixture is ready, add the noodles, cucumber, three-quarters of the beans sprouts, and the lime juice. Season with salt to taste, then bring back to a simmer. Add the shrimp and mussels and cook for 3 to 5 minutes – the shrimp should turn a pretty pink color and all the mussels should open – discard any mussels that don't open during cooking. Now stir in half of the shredded basil and mint, and mix the remaining herbs with the chopped nuts. Finally, ladle the soup into deep bowls, sprinkle with the remaining bean sprouts and the herb-nut mixture, and serve.

Stilton Soup with Parmesan Croutons
Serves 4 to 6

4 tablespoons butter

1 onion, finely chopped

1 leek, white and pale green part only, chopped and well rinsed

1 large baking potato, such as russet or Burbank, peeled and cut into ½-inch dice

1½ tablespoons all-purpose flour

⅔ cup hard cider

2¼ cups Chicken Stock (page 128)

1¼ cups milk

4 oz Stilton, shedded

1 tablespoon heavy cream

Salt and freshly ground black pepper to taste

Parmesan Croutons (page 129)

This stunning recipe is a great way to use your best Stilton. The creamy soup is very rich, so serve in small cups. While the soup can be made in advance, it needs to be reheated slowly so that it never boils, or the cheese will separate.

1. Start off by melting the butter in a large, heavy-bottomed saucepan, then add the onion, leek, and potato, with some salt. Cover and cook gently for 5 to 10 minutes to draw out the juices. Next, stir in the flour to absorb the juices, and when it reaches a smooth consistency, gradually pour in the cider – still stirring. Now add the chicken stock, cover again, and simmer gently until the potatoes are tender, about 30 minutes.

2. Once the 30 minutes are up, add the milk and Stilton to the saucepan and heat, stirring, until the cheese has melted and the soup is just below the boiling point. Taste and season with salt and pepper, then stir in the cream and let the soup cool a bit. At this stage, you can purée it in a blender or food processor in batches (pour the puréed soup into a bowl) – or, if you prefer the texture of the chopped vegetables, keep it as it is. Serve the soup with the Parmesan croutons.

Flemish Potato and Leek Soup with Brussels Sprouts
Serves 4 to 6

2 medium (12 oz) baking potatoes, such as russet or Burbank

2 large leeks, white and pale green parts only

12 oz Brussels sprouts

4 tablespoons butter

Salt and freshly ground black pepper

2 cups Vegetable Stock (page 128)

2 cups milk

3 tablespoons crème fraîche or heavy cream

A squeeze of fresh lemon juice

4 tablespoons crème fraîche or heavy cream, for serving

For the crispy sprouts

4 large Brussels sprouts, trimmed and shredded

1 tablespoon olive oil

Brussels sprouts heighten considerably in flavor after a hard frost. The large, fat, open-textured ones are too big for serving but they are just perfect for making this classic Flemish soup. So creamy and subtle is it that even determined sprouts haters have been known to succumb to its charms. If you want to make the crispy sprouts garnish in advance, you can reheat it in a skillet just before serving.

1. Start by peeling and thickly slicing the potatoes. Next, make a vertical split about halfway down the center of each leek and clean them by running them under cold water while you fan out the layers - this will rid them of any hidden dust and grit. Now slice them in half lengthways and chop into 1-inch pieces. Then trim the bases of the sprouts and discard any damaged outer leaves, and quarter the larger sprouts and halve any smaller ones. Next, melt the butter in a large saucepan, add the potatoes, leeks, and sprouts, and stir well to coat them nicely in the butter. Add some salt and pepper, turn the heat to low, cover, and let the vegetables cook gently for 5 minutes. Then add the stock and milk, bring everything up to a simmer, and cook very gently for 20 to 25 minutes, or until the potatoes are soft. To keep the milk from boiling over, it's best to leave the lid ajar and to keep the heat really low.

2. After that, cool the soup a bit. In batches, purée it in a blender or food processor, pouring the puréed soup into a large bowl. Return the soup to the saucepan. Add the crème fraîche, then reheat the soup gently, taste, and add a good squeeze of lemon juice and more seasoning, if it needs it.

3. Meanwhile, make the garnish while the soup is reheating. To do this, heat the olive oil in a small skillet over high heat. When the oil is really hot and shimmering, add the shredded sprouts and fry them, stirring occasionally, so they don't stick to the bottom of the skillet. When they are crisp and golden brown – which should take 2 to 3 minutes – use a slotted spoon to transfer them to crumpled paper towels to drain. Serve the soup in hot bowls with a little crème fraîche spooned on top of each one and garnished with the crispy sprouts.

Slow-Cooked Root Vegetable Soup
Serves 6

4 medium carrots (8 oz), cut into 2-inch lengths

1 small celery root (8 oz), pared and into 2-inch pieces

2 medium leeks, white and pale green parts only, well washed, halved lengthwise, and cut into 2-inch lengths (8 oz cleaned weight)

½ medium waxed yellow rutabaga, pared, and cut into 2-inch pieces (8 oz cleaned weight)

1 small onion, roughly chopped

6 cups Vegetable Stock (page 128)

3 bay leaves

Salt and freshly ground black pepper to taste

Plain yogurt, for garnish

Snipped fresh chives, for garnish

When root vegetables are cooked very slowly for a long time, something special happens to them: their flavor becomes both more intense and more mellow at the same time. A proper balance of vegetables contributes to the final result, so weights are provided to weigh them at the market, if you don't happen to have a kitchen scale.

1. Preheat the oven to 275°F. There's not much to do here once everything is peeled and chopped. All you do is put everything in a large flameproof casserole with a cover. Add a seasoning of salt and pepper and bring it to a gentle simmer on top of the stove. Cover the casserole, place it in the lower third of the oven, and cook undisturbed for 3 hours, by which time the vegetables will be meltingly tender.

2. Let the soup cool awhile. Remove the bay leaves. In batches, purée the soup in a blender or food processor, pouring the puréed soup into a bowl. Return the soup to the saucepan and gently reheat it. Serve the soup in bowls with a spoonful of yogurt swirled into each and garnished with the fresh chives.

Polish-Style Beet Soup
with Pumpernickel Croutons
Serves 4 to 6

For the stock

1 tablespoon peanut or other
flavorless oil, as needed

9 oz pork neck with bones,
or pork chop

2 medium carrots, cut into chunks

1 large onion, roughly chopped

1 bay leaf

6 fresh parsley sprigs

Salt and freshly ground black
pepper to taste

For the stock

6 medium beets (2 lb 4 oz),
scrubbed but unpeeled

3 tablespoons butter, softened

4 teaspoons all-purpose flour

⅓ cup sour cream

3 tablespoons fresh lemon juice

Salt and freshly ground black
pepper to taste

Sour cream, for serving

Croutons, made with
pumpernickel bread (page 129)

Some beet soups, or borschts, are meatless; this one uses meat to make the stock, although the soup itself contains only beets. Served hot, garnished with sour cream, pumpernickel croutons, and grated beets, this puréed soup tastes as brilliant as it looks.

1. First of all, you need to make a stock: heat the oil in a large saucepan, and when it's really hot, in batches, add the pork, carrot, and onion, and cook them, keeping the heat high and adding more oil as needed, until they're brownish-black at the edges. This is important because it gives the stock a good flavor. When you're happy with the color, about 6 minutes per batch, return everything to the saucepan and add 7 cups water, the bay leaf, and parsley, followed by a good seasoning of salt and pepper. As soon as it begins to simmer, turn the heat down and simmer very gently, uncovered, for 40 minutes. After that, strain it through a sieve into a bowl, throw out the solids, and rinse the saucepan to use again.

2. While the stock is cooking, you can deal with the beets. Place them in another saucepan, add enough boiling water to barely cover them, and add a pinch of salt. Cover and simmer gently for 40 minutes or until tender when pierced with a skewer. Drain the beets, then cover them with cold water to cool them. As soon as they're cool enough to handle, slip off the skin. Shred 1 beet for the garnish and cut the rest into cubes. Put the cubed beets in the stock saucepan, add the stock, and bring to a simmer. Cover and simmer gently for 20 minutes.

3. Mash the butter and flour together into a paste in a small bowl. Using a slotted spoon, transfer half of the beets from the soup to a blender or food processor. Add the paste and purée the beets, adding some of the soup liquid as you go. Pour the borscht into a large bowl. Repeat with the remaining beets and the sour cream, return to the saucepan, and add the borscht in the bowl. Add the lemon juice, check the seasoning, and reheat gently. Serve the soup in warmed soup bowls, swirl in the sour cream, and scatter the croutons and shredded beet on top.

Hungarian Goulash Soup with Dumplings and Sour Cream

Serves 4 to 6

1 lb beef chuck or round steak

1–2 tablespoons olive oil

1 large onion, finely chopped

1 tablespoon all-purpose flour

2 tablespoons Hungarian hot paprika, plus a little extra for sprinkling

½ teaspoon caraway seeds

¼ teaspoon dried marjoram (optional)

1 garlic clove, chopped

6 cups Beef Stock or Vegetable Stock (page 128)

One (14 oz) can chopped tomatoes

1 teaspoon tomato paste

3 medium baking potatoes, such as russet or Burbank, peeled and cut into ½-inch dice

1 green or red bell pepper, seeds and ribs removed, chopped

Salt and freshly ground black pepper to taste

Sour cream, for serving

For the dumplings

1 cup all-purpose flour, plus a little extra for sprinkling

1 teaspoon baking powder

2 oz suet (or vegetable shortening), chilled and shredded on a box grater

Salt and freshly ground black pepper

Billowing dumplings afloat on a stew of beef, tomatoes, and spicy paprika, mellowed with sour cream – this is a great winter warmer. It's a meal in a bowl, so no need for anything besides bread and cheese to follow.

1. Begin by trimming and cutting the beef into ½-inch cubes. Then heat the oil in a large flameproof saucepan. In batches, add the beef and cook over high heat until well browned, transferring it to a plate when browned. Now stir in the onion, adding a little extra oil if needed. Cook the onion over medium heat for about 5 minutes or until it's lightly browned, stirring now and then. Then return the meat to the casserole and sprinkle in the flour, paprika, caraway, marjoram, if using, and garlic. Season with salt. Stir well and cook for a minute before adding the stock and tomatoes. When it comes to a simmer, cover and simmer very gently for 45 minutes.

2. After that, uncover and stir in the tomato paste, followed by the potatoes and green pepper. Bring the goulash back to a simmer and cook gently, covered, for 10 minutes, stirring occasionally.

3. To make the dumplings, mix the flour and baking powder in a bowl, and add the suet. Season with salt and pepper, and stir in enough cold water (6–8 tablespoons) to make a smooth dough. Transfer the dough to a lightly floured board and shape into 12 small balls. Pop them onto the soup – don't press them down, though, just let them float. Then put the cover back on and simmer for 25 minutes more. Taste to check the seasoning, and ladle the goulash into six warmed, deep bowls, making sure everyone has at least 2 dumplings. Finish each one with a spoonful of sour cream and a sprinkling of paprika.

Yellow Split Pea Soup
Serves 6

2 quarts Ham Stock or Vegetable Stock (page 128)

2 scant cups yellow or green split peas (no need to soak)

6 tablespoons butter

6 slices bacon, diced

1 medium onion, coarsely chopped

1 medium celery stalk, chopped

1 large carrot, sliced

Salt and freshly ground black pepper to taste

To serve

Crispy bacon bits (see recipe)

3 slices firm white sandwich bread, crusts trimmed, cut into ⅓-inch cubes

Smoky bacon flavors this thick, hearty soup, which is served with croutons and more bacon, crisped and crumbled into bits. If you have a stick blender, you can purée the peas right in the pot, rather than in batches in a blender or food processor.

1. First of all, pour the stock into your largest saucepan and bring just to a simmer. Add the split peas, stir well, and simmer very gently for about 30 minutes. Meanwhile, heat 2 tablespoons of the butter in a medium saucepan. Add two-thirds of the bacon, along with the onion, celery, and carrot. Cook them over medium heat until softened and nicely golden – this will take about 15 minutes.

2. After that, transfer the bacon and vegetables to the split peas. Then add some salt and pepper, cover, and simmer very gently for 40 to 50 minutes, or until the peas are very tender.

3. Meanwhile, heat a large empty skillet over medium heat. Add the remaining bacon and cook until it is really crisp. Using a slotted spoon, transfer the bacon to a plate. Next add 2 tablespoons of the butter to the pan, and as soon as it begins to foam, add the bread cubes. Fry the bread cubes, tossing them around in the skillet, for about 5 minutes, or until they are also nice and crisp.

4. When the soup is ready, let it cool a little. In batches, purée the soup in a blender or food processor, pouring the soup into a large bowl. Return the puréed soup to the saucepan. Taste to check the seasoning, and add a little more stock or water if it seems too thick. Just before serving, add the remaining butter, and stir the soup until the butter melts. Ladle the soup into serving bowls, and sprinkle each one with the croutons and crispy bacon bits.

Stocks and Garnishes

High-quality fresh or frozen stocks are sometimes available at well-stocked supermarkets, but they can be expensive. It's easy and much better to make your own. Miso is a useful pantry item for a quick stock (see pages 22 and 33) for Asian soups. Here's how to make a few basic stocks – once cooled, they can all be refrigerated or frozen.

Beef Stock
Makes about 9 cups

For a light beef stock, use the same ingredients and follow the same instructions but leave out the initial roasting of the bones and vegetables.

3 lb beef bones, sawed into 3-inch pieces
2 large carrots, peeled and cut into chunks
2 medium onions, quartered
3 medium celery ribs, each cut into three pieces
1 teaspoon salt
A few fresh parsley stalks
1 sprig of fresh thyme
1 blade of mace (optional)
8 whole black peppercorns
1 bay leaf

1. Preheat the oven to 450°F. Begin by placing the bones in a large roasting pan, tucking the carrots, onions, and celery among the bones. Do not add any fat. Place the pan in the upper third of the oven and roast for 45 minutes, basting with the juices now and then. After that, the bones and the vegetables will have turned brown at the edges.

2. Now transfer them all to the very largest saucepan you own and add enough cold water just to cover everything - about 12 cups. Add the rest of the ingredients, then as soon as it reaches boiling point, skim off the foam and lower the heat. Put the lid on, but not completely since it's best to leave a little gap for the steam to escape, which will help to reduce and concentrate the stock as it simmers. Let the stock cook very gently on a low heat for about 4 hours.

3. Remove the stock from the heat, and let stand until cool. Then refrigerate until cold. Using a slotted spoon, remove the fat that will have congealed on the surface. The stock is now ready to use.

Chicken Stock
Makes about 2 quarts

2 pounds chicken wings,
chopped between the joints

2 medium celery ribs with leaves, split
lengthwise and cut in half crosswise

2 medium carrots, split lengthwise

2 medium onions, sliced

8 fresh parsley stalks

12 whole black peppercorns

2 bay leaves

A pinch of salt

Place the all the ingredients in a large saucepan with 10 cups cold water and bring to the boil. Skim off any foam, and simmer briskly for 1 hour. Strain the stock. Cool, refrigerate, and remove any congealed fat from the surface.

Ham Stock
Makes about 2 quarts

3 smoked ham hocks

2 medium celery ribs with leaves

1 large carrot, split lengthwise

1 large leek, split lengthwise

A few fresh parsley stalks

1 sprig of fresh thyme

6 whole black peppercorns

1 bay leaf

Place all of the ingredients in a large saucepan and add 10 cups cold water. Bring everything to a simmer and remove any foam from the surface. Simmer gently, partially covered, for 1½ to 2 hours. Strain, cool, and refrigerate the stock. Remove any fat from the surface.

Fish Stock
Makes about 3 cups

1 lb fish trimmings from white-fleshed fish
(no gills), well rinsed

⅔ cup dry white wine

1 small onion, quartered

2 medium celery ribs, chopped

a few sprigs of fresh parsley

1 sprig fresh thyme

1 bay leaf

Salt and freshly ground black pepper to taste

Place all of the ingredients in the pan with 9 cups cold water and bring to a simmer. Skim off any foam and simmer uncovered for about 20 minutes. Strain, cool, and refrigerate until ready to use.

Shellfish Stock

Make as above, substituting the shells of 1 lb shrimp for the fish trimmings.

Vegetable Stock
Makes about 6 cups

3 medium celery ribs with leaves, split
lengthwise and cut in half crosswise

5 small carrots, split lengthways

4 small onions, sliced

12 fresh parsley stalks

12 whole black peppercorns

2 bay leaves

A pinch of salt

Place all the ingredients in a large saucepan with 7 cups cold water. Bring to a boil, cover, and boil briskly for 30 minutes. Strain, discarding the vegetables. Cool before storing.

Croutons
Serves 4

Crisp, golden croutons are lovely sprinkled over the top of a bowl of hot or chilled soup. You can make croutons a day ahead, and store them in an airtight container once they have cooled.

2–3 slices firm, white bread,
cut into ½-inch cubes

1 tablespoon olive oil

Preheat the oven to 350°F. Place the bread in a bowl, drizzle with the oil, and stir so the cubes get an even coating. Spread them on a baking sheet. Bake in the upper third of the oven for 10 minutes, or until the croutons are crisp and golden. One word of warning: use a kitchen timer for this operation because it's actually very hard to bake something for just 10 minutes without forgetting all about it. Cool on the baking sheet.

Garlic Croutons
Serves 4

Follow the recipe for plain croutons (above), only this time add 1 crushed garlic clove to the bowl with the bread cubes and oil. Stir together and bake as above for 10 minutes (remember to put a timer on). Cool and store in an airtight container until you are ready to use them.

Parmesan Croutons
Serves 4

Follow the recipe for plain croutons (left), stirring the bread cubes and oil in a small bowl until the oil is soaked up. Sprinkle with 1 tablespoon freshly grated Parmesan and stir again until coated. Bake as above.

Olive Croutons
Serves 4

4 slices crusty Italian bread

1 tablespoon olive oil

2 teaspoons olive paste, such as olivada or tapenade

1. Preheat the oven to 375°F. Cut the sliced bread into ½-inch cubes. Then place the bread in a bowl, together with the oil and olive paste. Stir until the cubes get a good coating of the olive oil paste.

2. Next, spread the bread cubes on a baking sheet and bake for 8 to 10 minutes – remember to set the kitchen timer. Cool the croutons on the baking sheet. Store in an airtight container until you are ready to use them.

Other Ideas

Here are a few other quick and easy suggestions that you might like to try when serving soups.

Add a spoonful of freshly snipped chives or other herbs, or some finely chopped hot chilies or scallions (including the green tops), to the bottom of each bowl before ladling in soup, or sprinkle onto each bowl as a garnish before serving.

A marbling of heavy cream, crème fraîche, or yogurt (particularly if you are watching the calories) can be swirled in just before you're ready to serve hot or chilled soup.

Plenty of freshly grated Parmesan cheese or slices of crusty French bread, topped with a melting cheese, such as Fontina or Gruyère, then browned under the broiler, are lovely additions to warming winter soups.

Brussels sprouts, shallots, and leeks are delicious finely shredded and then lightly fried in a little oil in a very hot skillet before sprinkling over soups.

Smoked bacon or pancetta, cut into cubes or sliced thinly, then fried until crisp and golden, make another excellent garnish.

Salsas or paper-thin slices of cucumber or fruit, such as apple or halved grapes, are a nice idea, especially when you're making low-fat soups.

Vegetable Chips

If you're entertaining, chips made with root vegetables, such as parsnips or sweet potato, are a rather special garnish for hot soups.

1 medium to large parsnip or sweet potato
6 tablespoons peanut or other flavorless oil
Salt

1. First, peel the parsnip or sweet potato and then slice it into rounds as thinly as you possibly can, using a sharp knife or a mandoline, which is ideal for this job. Now heat the oil in a large skillet until it is very hot, almost smoking. Fry the slices in batches until they are golden brown, about 2 to 3 minutes. They will not stay flat or color evenly but will twist into lovely shapes (see right).

2. As they're cooked, transfer them with a slotted spoon to paper towels to drain. Sprinkle lightly with salt. If you like, you can make these in advance, because they will stay crisp for a couple of hours.

Equipment

You don't need a lot of special equipment for making soups at home except for a food processor, blender, or alternatively, a hand-held blender. A blender is excellent for puréeing smooth, elegant soups whereas a food processor is fine when you want to have a bit of texture in the soup.

Crème Fraîche

Makes about 1 cup

Crème fraîche is a luxuriously rich, thick cream that won't curdle when added to hot liquids (unlike sour cream which is too tangy to be a good substitute, anyway), so it is especially useful when making soup. As crème fraîche is not available at every market, here is a homemade version.

¾ cup plus 2 tablespoons heavy cream, preferably not ultra-pasteurized

2 tablespoons buttermilk

1. Whisk the cream and buttermilk together in a small saucepan. Stir over low heat until the mixture feels just warmer than body temperature (dip your clean finger into the saucepan to check). Pour the mixture into a very clean, glass jar with a lid. Cover loosely with plastic wrap. Let stand and room temperature until the crème fraîche thickens, about 24 hours.

2. Cover the crème fraîche jar with its lid and refrigerate for another 24 hours, where it will continue to thicken and develop more flavor. It will keep, refrigerated, for up to 2 weeks.

Index

Picture credits

Steve Baxter 83
Jean Cazals 34, 110
Patrice de Villiers 102
Miki Duisterhof 5, 6, 14/15, 23, 28, 34, 38, 60, 64, 68, 76, 89, 93, 94, 118, 121, 131, 133
Norman Hollands 71
Peter Knab 6, 10, 13, 16, 19, 20, 23, 30/31, 34, 42, 48, 52, 56, 59, 67, 71, 89, 94, 98, 101, 105, 117, 126
Jonathan Lovekin 27, 34, 52, 113
Jason Lowe 101
J P Masclet 137
S & O Matthews 6, 28, 34, 60, 79, 94
Gareth Morgans 23, 28, 83, 89, 131
David Munns 76, 117, 126
Debbie Patterson 84/85
Michael Paul 24, 41, 72
Dan Stevens 60, 90
Kevin Summers 60, 94
Simon Walton 9, 10, 32, 38, 45, 52, 55, 59, 63, 80, 86, 101, 106, 110, 122, 131
Cameron Watt 6, 16, 28, 37, 38, 46/47, 51, 52, 59, 71, 74/75, 83, 89, 94, 97, 108/9, 110, 114, 117, 125
Rob White 10, 64, 76, 117
Tim Winter 6, 34, 94

Delia Smith is an international culinary phenomenon, whose best-selling cookbooks have sold over 17 million copies.

Delia's other books include *How To Cook Books One, Two,* and *Three,* her *Vegetarian Collection,* the *Complete Illustrated Cookery Course, One Is Fun,* the *Summer* and *Winter Collections,* and *Christmas.* Delia is the creator of Canary Catering and now runs five successful restaurants and a series of regular food and wine workshops.

She is married to the writer and editor Michael Wynn Jones and they live in England.

Visit Delia's website at www.deliaonline.com